THE CAPTIVE WIFE

THE CAPTIVE WIFE
Conflicts of Housebound Mothers

HANNAH GAVRON

ROUTLEDGE & KEGAN PAUL
LONDON, BOSTON, MELBOURNE AND HENLEY

First published in 1966
New edition with New Introduction published in 1983 by
Routledge & Kegan Paul plc,
39 Store Street, London WC1E 7DD,
9 Park Street, Boston, Mass. 02108, USA,
464 St Kilda Road, Melbourne,
Victoria 3004, Australia and
Broadway House, Newtown Road,
Henley-on-Thames, Oxon. RG9 1EN
Printed in Great Britain by
Billing & Sons Ltd., Worcester

ISBN 0-7102-0035-8

CONTENTS

Contents

NEW INTRODUCTION
BY ANN OAKLEY

In the end we also will be dead, and our own lives will lie inert within the finished process, our intentions assimilated within a past event which we never intended. What we may hope is that men and women of the future will reach back to us, will affirm and renew our meanings, and make our history intelligible within their own present tense. They alone will have the power to select from the many meanings offered by our quarrelling present, and to transmit some part of our process into their progress (Thompson, 1978,[1] p. 234).

Hannah Gavron was born in 1936 and died from suicide before her thirtieth birthday. *The Captive Wife* was her only book, though by no means her only published work,[2] and she did not live to see it published, to assess people's reactions to it or to follow through what many who read it felt to be its great promise. *The Captive Wife* stands on its own, intensely quoted and commented on, but ultimately tantalising in what it does *not* say, in what it is *not* able to tell us about its own conception, gestation and birth, and about the regard in which its author held it and herself. There is also the distracting and unanswerable question as to in which of many possible directions Hannah Gavron would have taken the book's pioneering trails had she lived; of what more complete understanding of women's existence and family life we have been deprived by her death.

---

[1] Bibliographic references in this New Introduction are to the Additional Bibliography on page 171.
[2] She was a regular contributor of book reviews to *The Economist* and *New Society*.

New Introduction

The book began as a PhD thesis under the supervision of Professor Ronald Fletcher at Bedford College, University of London. Gavron obtained her doctorate in 1965, and the empirical part of her thesis consisted of ninety-six interviews carried out by Gavron herself with young married mothers in North London. (The aim was a hundred, so that no percentages need be calculated, but weariness, quite understandably, took over.) Since social class was to be an important parameter of the analysis, the sample was divided equally into working class and middle class, according to the prevailing British definition of social class in terms of male occupation. The resulting data appear in the middle, largest section of *The Captive Wife*, prefaced by a section on the historical background and location of the survey, and followed by a more interpretative conclusion and methodological appendices. The main section of the book describes how the women in Gavron's sample responded to a series of questions, delivered using a mixed structured and unstructured interviewing approach, to nine topics of areas ranging from 'The Home' to 'Organization of Family Life' and 'Work'.

The Captive Wife has two different sets of origins and audiences. These, like the proverbial in-laws, jostle uncomfortably with one another behind a plastic façade of good relations. On the one hand, there are the sociologists, the earnest investigators of a phenomenon called family life, who collectively spawned, in the 1950s and 1960s in Britain, a veritable fishpond of studies tracking the relationships between the private life of families and the public life of communities. In books such as Mogey's *Family and Neighbourhood* (1956), Dennis, Henriques and Slaughter's *Coal is Our Life* (1956) and Young and Willmott's *Family and Kinship in East London* (1957), a facilely romanticized picture emerged of large, three-generation working class families which were truly havens in a heartless world—or seemed so, to the (often male) academically alienated, middle class sociologists. Gavron addressed herself directly to this same sociological enterprise of uncovering the social reality of family relations. Indeed, she identified Young and Willmott's book as the 'starting point' for her own research, and said that what she wanted to do was to explore Young and Willmott's conclusions in an area that was not one of middle-aged 1950s poverty, but rather one of young 1960s affluence— the 'never-had-it-so-good' ethos of a full employment, consumer society. *The Captive Wife*'s other set of origins are in the nature of poor and less visible relations. It *is* a book about the position of women, and Gavron was undoubtedly at least as interested in this as in the fate and functions of the family. In the first sentence of her own Introduction Gavron states in no uncertain terms that 'This is a study about women. . . .' Reflecting on the apparent disappearance of feminism in the years since the suffragettes, she asks, 'Have all the great changes in the position of women in the last 150 years come to nothing?' 'The only way to begin to answer this', she determines, 'is to study women themselves . . .' —an exercise which meant, in terms of the interviewing process, being concerned 'above all to discover the respondents' *own* perceptions of their situation'. Returning to the subjectivity of people's own experiences, disrespecting grand theory, and grounding interpretations of the world on the unpretentious basis of the lives lived in it—these practices were to become in the succeeding decade the new tenets of a new brand of sociological theory—ethnomethodology—and of a newly self-conscious field of *feminist* research. But feminism, its second great twentieth-century wave, was not yet born when Gavron started work on *The Captive Wife*, and this fact makes the book itself both more remarkable and more limited: a child both of its time and, like the heroine of Marge Piercy's *Woman on the*

New Introduction

Edge of Time (1979), one perched on the edge of it, possessed of that leap-frogging imagination that is the peculiar gift and fragile sanity of the marginal.

The 1950s and early 1960s in Britain and many other countries were hardly years of overt feminist debate. The cultural atmosphere, as Elizabeth Wilson (1980) has argued, seemed to encode a glassy silence on the subject of women. There *were* those who spoke—Simone de Beauvoir in *The Second Sex* (1949), Mirra Komarovsky in *Women in the Modern World* (1953), Viola Klein in *The Feminine Character* (1946) and with Alva Myrdal in *Women's Two Roles* (1956)—and to the extent that the *possibility* of women's protest about their situation is held permanently within the structure of industrial capitalism, the lines of communication never really went dead. Yet there was no women's movement in post-war Britain, no generalised recognition of that conflict and ambivalence which Gavron laid bare in *The Captive Wife*. And in so far as women constituted academic subject-matter, they were caught in the still landscape of the problem they posed for *men*, in the classic formulae of 'working wives' and 'maternal deprivation', neither of which allowed for the problematic of women's own needs.

As a sociologist of her time Gavron is suspended uneasily in the air of these traditional sexist debates. She asks the question as to whether women's employment threatens family stability and answers no; she inquires as to whether children may be damaged or made delinquent by employed mothers, and finds no evidence for supposing that they are. The point is both that she addresses the question in its own terms and senses the irrelevance of these terms to the different panorama of dilemmas unveiled by her interviewees. It is important to bear in mind here that any radical reformulation of the question would have been strongly resisted by the sociological milieu within which Gavron worked. In this

x

sense, sociology has never fulfilled the promise of being a truly 'social' science: only at odd moments has it managed to reflect the social realities of the two genders at all equally. The vantage points of women have been trivialised by being set within a 'social problem' perspective, by a gross visibility in family sociology, and by an almost total invisibility in other sociological domains. The entrenched hostility of sociologists to the social importance of women was the reason why, when I myself came to follow in Gavron's footsteps a decade later by carrying out a study of women's attitudes to housework (Oakley, 1974a, 1974b), I found it necessary to preface my main report of that study with a chapter on the invisibility of women in sociology. It was more than the intellectual context in which I worked; it was itself the obstacle to be overcome. The fact that I had enormous difficulty in 1969 in securing an academic supervisor for my work who would be prepared to understand and accept *my* definition of its subject (housework *as work*) suggests to me that Gavron's own path some years before had probably been even rougher.

I never met Hannah Gavron, but our lives touched each other's and have run in parallel lines in several important ways. Our parents knew one another; I was an undergraduate with her younger sister who subsequently became a close friend. When I left university, one of my first jobs was to work for Gavron's father, T.R. Fyvel, on a study of higher education. My research and PhD were done, like hers, at Bedford College, and sprang, like hers, initially from the well of my own personal experience. When I came to seek a publisher for my own work in the early 1970s, Routledge appropriately rejected my manuscript on the grounds that they had published Gavron's, and there could be no room on the publishing scene for more than *one* book about housewives. But most important is my intellectual debt to her; simply for having *succeeded* in doing the research for, and writing, *The Captive Wife*. The importance (on both intellectual and purely practical levels) of successful role models for women in the professions has been attested by many pieces of research. Hannah Gavron held that position for me. Certainly, in practical terms, during my own struggle single-handedly to carry out a series of demanding interviews when my own first two children were still pre-school, I could but admire Gavron's achievements in making it through that magic number of ninety-six. Her suicide, which came almost at the very moment of her success, could hardly have been unrelated to the dilemmas and contradictions of women's situation which have been part of professional subject matter for both of us. Private issues of autonomy, dependence and self-esteem, which are central to women's socialisation as women, are not necessarily adequately sidestepped by a succession of achievements in the public world. As one of the insights of that genus of work inspired by *The Captive Wife*, we now understand that what many women may have individually known in relation to these internal unsolved problems is very much in the nature of a shared destiny.

Routledge's predictions about the publishing scene have, fortunately, been proved wrong. Since 1970 there has been an explosion of books about, and for, women in almost every field and from a tremendous variety of perspectives. One consequence of this has been a re-evaluation of much earlier work on women's position, including *The Captive Wife*; for, as Edward Thompson in the quotation at the head of this Introduction says, the present has a tendency to reach back into the past and impose a new pattern on it, irrespective, almost, of what might have been intended then. Reading through the original reviews of *The Captive Wife*, one is struck by the character of the messages picked up as bright and new at the time. Typical headlines were 'Alone with the Gadgets' (*The Listener*), 'Prisoners in their own Home'

(*South Wales Echo*), 'The Loneliness of the Stay-at-home Mother' (*Evening Standard*), 'Walled- in Wives' (*Nova*), 'Are You Giving Your Wife a Square Deal?' (*Daily Sketch*) and 'Is Your Wife Just a Bird in a Plastic Cage?' (*Sunday Express*). What was appealed to was the notion of confinement, expressed as the social problem of *isolation*. Gavron herself gave a good deal of emphasis to this 'finding', relating the absence of street life and social contacts generally in her sample of working class wives to the opposed and dominant picture of working class sociability extant in the community studies literature. 'The young working class mother in this sample' states Gavron baldly 'was confined to her home. . . .' Deprived of the help and companionship of the socially cohesive and geographically stable extended family, she was thrown back on her own resources, on the resources of the neighbourhood. Poor housing, and a class-determined diffidence with respect to friendship, accounted for a high degree of isolation—25% of Gavron's working class sample (but none of the middle class women) said they had no friends.

If the media capitalised on the social isolation theme, they did so partly because this was a remediable feature of the problem. All sorts of practical solutions might be found—more organisations and community activities for mothers of young children, more out-of-home day-care for the under-fives, playrooms in department stores, helpful bus conductors unlikely to throw a fit at the sight of a woman overburdened with uncompliant babies and the entire contents of Mothercare. Yet the underlying problem without a name, so-called by Betty Friedan in *The Feminine Mystique* (1963), posed a much tougher conundrum. If women were in a state of conflict, ambivalent about the dual roles of worker and mother, if not exactly about those of wife and worker, then what could be done about it? Or, rather, could society really take on board any of the available

proposed solutions? The issue was nicely stated by
'Another Captive Wife' writing to the *Observer* news-
paper following that paper's publication of a review of
Gavron's book:

> My husband pointed out the article 'The Captive Wife',
> and said I should read it. I did so, and agreed with many
> of the problems mentioned. When I asked my husband
> what he had thought of it, he admitted he had not
> himself read it. . . .
>
> My husband is very nice. He has no objection to
> women working, and praises some who do it well. He
> does not even mind if I work, but he does not care
> tuppence if I don't. He does not even care that I cannot
> work because of our children, although I want to do so.
> He regards this as an understandable wish, like wanting
> a holiday in Greece, but not as a need that society is
> under an obligation to notice, like old age pensions.
>
> I do not say that this attitude is wrong—or right. The
> point is, my husband is a personnel manager. (*Observer
> Weekend Review*, 8 May 1966)

The calm tone of the letter belies its underlying anger.
Men could approve of the existence of *The Captive Wife*
but intransigently resume their traditional stance. 'What
do women want?' asked the *Church Times* reviewer
impatiently. 'What does the emancipation of women
really mean?' inquired Keith Thomas in the *New
Statesman*. But mostly the response to the book did not
identify it with a serious epistemological quest to
uncover the essential humanity, the personhood, of
women. This was the mantle bestowed on it by the
succeeding, and more explicitly feminist, genus of
literature on the problem without a name that came,
eventually, to acquire an embarrassing, even contradic-
tory, prolificity of *different* names.

The Captive Wife sold almost 5000 copies in five years
in the UK and 46,930 copies in twelve months in Japan, a

country apparently greedy for books on housebound women. By publishing standards it did well, and in intellectual terms it preceded a whole generation of studies on women's captivity and immersion in the business of daily manufacturing successful homes, labouring husbands, and surviving children. There are now histories of housework such as Caroline Davidson's *A Woman's Work is Never Done* (1982) for Britain and Susan Strasser's *Never Done* (1982) for the United States. There are accounts of the evolution and status of domestic service, such as Leonore Davidoff's *The Best Circles* (1973) and Theresa McBride's *The Domestic Revolution* (1976). There are serious and comprehensive collections of essays on household work (*Women and Household Labour*, edited by Sarah Fenstermaker Berk, 1980). Many women have, since those pioneering days, talked to other women about housework and marriage and childcare (see, for example, Ginsberg, 1976; Hobson, 1978; Lopata, 1971. Housework has been dignified by its inclusion in the Marxist rhetoric (for instance, Barrett, 1980; Secombe, 1973), although there remains a healthy disagreement within this discourse about just what housework is. Capitalist development may provoke a segmentation of personal life as the property of women (Zaretsky, 1976), but everyone (almost) is now prepared to recognise that what house-work is above all is *More Than a Labour of Love* (Luxton, 1980).

To single out for serious study, and thus elevate, the work of women at home was not part of Hannah Gavron's plan in *The Captive Wife*. However, by commenting on every other aspect of women's domestic situation, she succeeded, by default, as it were, in drawing attention to a cavernous gap in our knowledge of 'family' life. Some of her data and conclusions may have been challenged since (particularly those relating to men's roles in the home; see, for example, McKee, 1982), yet there is an inevitability about the criticism targetted at such trail-blazing studies as hers. By refocusing our gaze on a widening horizon, they generate a dialectic of debate which is by nature self-critical. Only thus is a new map of the world produced. Women in 1983 have a map of the world they didn't have in 1966; and it is our perpetual historical debt to Hannah Gavron that, whatever she may have intended at the time, her early endeavours in charting the contours of women's captivity helped to fashion a new way of seeing the world. Of course, not all the implications of our altered gaze have been worked out, and fewer still have reached the stage of social or academic acceptability. But that, again, merely testifies to the transcendentality of the original re-vision; and to the enormity of the work even now waiting to be done.

PREFACE
AND ACKNOWLEDGEMENTS

THIS book for the general reader is derived from a more technical thesis based on research work for a doctorate at London University, and a brief personal explanation may therefore be in place. The general shortcomings of the book are those of its author, but my work was also governed by the specific limitations imposed on a single researcher working without large funds or a supporting organization. In such circumstances, ambitions have to be severely restrained, large-scale generalizations are not called for, and this survey could therefore be regarded as an attempt to throw some light on some of the problems under investigation so as to reveal them more clearly and perhaps provide pointers for further investigations.

I am indebted to many people who gave help and advice in the course of the work and I wish particularly to offer my grateful thanks to the following: Professor Lady Williams, Professor Ronald Fletcher, Mr Peter Willmott, Dr Mark Abrams, Dr Elizabeth Bott, Mr T. R. Fyvel, Dr Hugh Faulkner, Dr Nicholas Rea, Dr Antony Ryle, Dr Donald Grant, Mrs Anne Wicks, Mrs Judy Price, Mr Stanley Price, Mrs Elizabeth Hall. For the faults of this work I must, of course, take full responsibility. I should also like to register especial thanks to Mrs Patricia Barkess for her help in sharing the care of my children—without her my work might have suffered many a delay. Above all, I owe thanks to my husband, Robert Gavron, for his invaluable help, encouragement and support.

London,
November, 1965.   HANNAH GAVRON

INTRODUCTION

THIS is a study about women, and in particular about young women with young children. But it is also intended to throw some more light on patterns of family life in the two social classes. In fact the starting point for this research was the desire to test further the findings of studies such as *Family and Kinship in East London* (Young and Willmott, 1951). This work highlighted the importance of the extended family and showed this to be the main source of wider social contact for working class families. It provided the main doorway to friendship and was maintained in particular by the relationship between 'Mum' and her married daughter. The close relationship between extended families was already well known to those who were concerned with the rehousing of people from slum areas, and Mogey in his study *Family & Neighbourhood* (1956) found the St. Ebbes families all part of extended networks, and very ill at ease when moved to new housing estates. But whereas the emphasis in the study by Young and Willmott had been on family relationships as a result of active choice, Mogey's study suggested that working class patterns of social contacts are by nature a *passive* acceptance of family and neighbourhood rather than an *active* selection of a circle of friends and contacts which involves a degree of social skill.

Many of the community studies carried out in the fifties had certain things in common:

1. All the studies were made in slum areas, or of people recently moved from slum neighbourhoods. But it might well be the case that extreme poverty produced a way of

life that was not by necessity shared by other sections of the working class who were more wealthy.

2. The studies were published in the middle fifties as a result of work done earlier. It could be said that they did not in any way cover the changes that had taken place in our society during the fifties.

3. The studies themselves—this is limited to the last point —were concerned on the whole with middle-aged people. It might well be that (a) family relationships are different in the early stages of marriage and (b) the newly married of the late fifties, who would themselves be members of the post-war generation might differ significantly from their parents.

It was possible, therefore, that these studies gave a portrait of certain kinds of working class life as it had been in the past. Even in *Family and Kinship in East London,* occasional hints were dropped that the younger married couples differed from their elders in certain ways, such as in the amount the fathers helped with their children. This was also noted by Shaw (1954) who found some evidence that attitudes and expectations of marriages held by young women differed from those held by women of previous generations. Certain key factors which these studies did not cover had to be taken into account. These were:

1. The 'young marrieds' of the fifties were members of a new mass society where success had come increasingly to be measured in terms of money and consumption. As Mark Abrams showed there was now a distinct pattern of teenage expenditure, concentrated on a whole range of products which were well publicised by the mass media.

2. Full employment had placed adolescent labour at a premium, and had given the contemporary working class family in particular a greater degree of financial security. There were signs that the old ties of working class solidarity might be weakening. Thus pressures on young people towards identification with the traditional values and norms of their parents might also have proved to be weaker.

3. The great increase in the employment of married women could have been expected to have an effect on family relationships, as many wives would now be released from complete financial dependence on their husbands.
4. The high wages that school leavers were able to obtain gave sons and daughters financial independence from their parents while in their teens.
5. The Welfare State now offered services for those events in life, for example childbirth, for which parents were once the only source of help and advice. Thus an alternative and more reliable source of guidance was available, which might in many cases differ completely from that proffered by 'Mum'.
6. The increased use of birth control brought a new freedom to married women which lessened the necessity for a 'Trade Union' of women to protect themselves from their men.
7. Increased employment meant increased wealth. Homes could be pleasanter and the husband would have more incentive to spend his leisure at home. He might therefore be drawn more easily into the general activities of the family.

It would appear reasonable to expect the combined effects of these changes to have some effect on family relationships among young couples, and to suspect that the lives of these young people had not yet been fully analysed.

At the same time another area of research seemed in need of extension. This was the impact of the changes in the position of women upon family life.

During this century, social, economic and technological changes have had a revolutionary effect on the status of women in this country, particularly working class women. With the industrial revolution men followed work from the home to the factory and women became dependent on men, not only in economic terms but also in terms of a whole pattern of psychological subtleties within their relationships. Authoritarian patterns of behaviour sanctioned in the factory were carried into the home. Also the survival of the family became increasingly dependent on the labour, power, health, strength and happiness of one person. Some of the changes which might be considered to have emancipated women from this authoritarian family structure are:

1. The revolution in child bearing brought about by increased use of birth control.
2. Legal changes in—divorce, the structure of property, care of children, and the extension of legal aid.
3. The vote giving equal political status with men.
4. Increased educational opportunity with the general expansion of education.
5. The increase in employment opportunities for married women.
6. The expansion of the social services which provide assistance and support to women at specific stages in their lives.
7. The importance of women to a 'consumer' society. This is also likely to have implications for the content of newspapers, magazines, television and other media.

By focusing this research on young wives, it was felt that any changes in working class family life would be encountered, and that the roles of young women within the modern family could be studied.

In particular it seemed that a study of young wives with at least one child would be of value because:

a. This would be a time when the wife is most dependent on her husband economically and socially. Thus any trends at this time towards an egalitarian relationship and the sharing of roles would be significant.

b. This might also be a time when young wives are most likely to turn to their mothers for assistance. Thus any evidence of lukewarm relationships particularly between working class wives and their 'Mums' would again suggest a difference from the patterns described above.

c. Then the ambitions, hopes, and expectations of the young women during this period when they are playing their traditional roles as wives and mothers might again reveal the status these women accord to themselves, the way in which *they* perceive their roles, and the way in which they relate themselves, both to their own families and to society in general.

At no stage was this intended to be a large scale statistical survey. It was to be a detailed study in depth of a small sample which would enable all the interviews to be carried out by one person. The result of such a concentrated analysis of a small sample would not of course provide evidence for any large scale generalisations but might provide an illuminating picture of the lives of the women studied. It would allow previous assumptions to be tested in detail, and would provide pointers for future research. By focusing on families from a normal London borough, with a good degree of variety in income and occupation, it might be possible to see to what extent relationships and patterns of behaviour differ from those presented in the books mentioned above.

As class differences have played an important role in British society, it was felt that any study of this nature ought to include a comparison between the middle class and the working class, with the main division coming between manual and non-manual (although some white collar working class have been included). This, it was thought, might prove to be particularly important at the present time, when many observers have suggested that patterns of family life among the two classes no longer show marked differences.

Thus the study covered two samples, working and middle class, with forty-eight wives in each sample.[1]

One final point needs to be made. This is a book that is specifically concerned with England and English society. While it is certainly true to say that present functions cannot always be explained in terms of historical origins, yet it remains equally true that our society is almost impossible to study, in however a limited form, without reference to the past. Where Family and Class are concerned the changes

[1] For details on the selection of the samples see Appendix III.

that have taken place over the last one hundred and fifty years are of vital importance, and this is just as true of the changes in women's roles. For this reason some historical background has been included, which is intended to provide a frame of reference for this study, and a starting point for relating its findings to more general issues.

PART ONE

Social and Historical Background

Chapter One

LEGAL AND POLITICAL
CHANGES

IT can be argued, said Geoffrey Gorer (1961) that 'Women of all classes were more exploited in the nineteenth century than in any previous period of European history.' Certainly, legally, politically, economically and socially women of the nineteenth century were second class citizens, subjected to the kinds of prejudices, conventions and restrictions that would be inconceivable to the young woman of today.

Any discussion of the position of women today must take into account the social revolution, as Titmuss has called it, of the last hundred years, if only to give a brief outline of those spheres of life where changes have occurred. 'The development,' says Titmuss, 'of personal legal and political liberties of half the population of the country within the span of less than eighty years stands as one of the supreme examples of consciously directed social change.' While it is debatable how fair it is to regard the emancipation of women as entirely the result of conscious forces, there is no doubt that effort and protest played an important part.

Any introductory background which seeks to chart the many changes in the position of women in this country must take into account three different, though interconnected, series of changes. Firstly the statutory changes in the position of women—primarily political, legal and economic. Secondly changes in the structure and scope of the family, and thirdly shifting patterns of class behaviour.

3

LEGAL EMANCIPATION

In 1837 the legal system reflected the prevailing attitudes towards women. At this time she had no vote, on marriage she and all her possessions including her children belonged to the husband under the 'fiction' of marital unity. If she left her husband he could force her to return, could refuse to support her, could refuse her access to her children.

Changes in the past hundred years extended the idea of separate use of property, and give married women parity with their single sisters. The first important landmark in this process was the Matrimonial Causes Act of 1857. This was essentially concerned with divorce, but also gave the first statutory act of protection for the property of married women, in that it allowed the separate use of any property acquired by a wife during a judicial separation or after a protection order on grounds of desertion. 1870 saw the Married Women's Property Act which allowed married women to receive independently beneficial interests in all their own earnings up to £200. The next important change came in 1882 with another Married Women's Property Act, when the husband's automatic rights to his wife's property on marriage were removed. The Matrimonial Causes Act of 1884 gave the wife rights over her own person, and the Law of Property Act of 1925 gave official recognition to the view that the husband and wife should be treated as two separate individuals in any property transaction. The Law Reform Act of 1935 and the Married Women (Restraint Upon Anticipation) Act of 1949 cleared away the last restrictions. At the same time changes in contract law were made to enable the wife to contract in her own name. Within the contract of marriage itself important changes also took place; as Graveson (1957) said 'the general concept of partnership' has come to replace that 'of principal agent or master and servant in relation to husband and wife'.

At the same time important changes took place with regard to parental rights and divorce. Before 1839 the father

4

had absolute rights over his children and even the Court of Chancery found it virtually impossible to grant a mother access to her children if her husband did not wish for this. The first change came in 1839 with the Custody of Infants Act which allowed some possibility of access though only under very special circumstances. Public opinion had been aroused by the granting of custody to the father of an eight month breast-fed baby. The 1857 Matrimonial Causes Act increased the possibilities of access and contact, and in 1873 the ban against mothers who had been established as adulterers was removed. With the Guardianship of Infants Act of 1886 the mother was permitted to be sole guardian of her children on her husband's death; and in 1891, the primacy of the child over the parents was acknowledged in an Act which permitted the Courts to grant custody of the child to the father only if he could satisfy the Court that he was in fact the best person to have this. This acknowledgement of the importance of the child, which in-directly served to benefit the mother, was underlined by another Act, the Guardianship of Infants Act of 1925, which stated that the welfare of the infant was to be of paramount importance, and thus the father could no longer have prior claims over the mother. (This process was con-tinued by a series of Acts between 1933 and 1952 to ensure adequate provision for children neglected or ill treated by parents.)

While the Matrimonial Causes Act of 1875 brought relief to women in many respects, it reinforced the double moral standard which discriminated against women. The divorce laws were based on the idea of the matrimonial offence— as they are today, and allowed the husband to sue on the grounds of adultery alone, but compelled the wife to plead cruelty as well. 1878 saw the Matrimonial Causes Act which gave the Courts power to make a separation order with maintenance for a wife whose husband had been convicted of assault on her, plus the custody of any children under ten. One of the crucial problems for all women without husbands was that of supporting themselves in a time that considered it against the essential nature of women to work. Thus the gradual legal enforcement of maintenance represented further improvements in the position of women. In 1886 an Act was passed which gave a wife who had brought a suit for the restitution of conjugal rights, the right to maintenance; and in 1866 husbands who deserted could be ordered to pay their wives a sum not exceeding £2 per week (till 1949 this ceiling remained the same). In 1889 an Act was passed permitting women who had ended the marriage the right to claim maintenance. At the same time the divorce laws were being altered slightly to improve the position of women. In 1895 a law was passed permitting a woman to request a separation order on the grounds of persistent cruelty by her husband, or his imprisonment for a period of more than two months. Thus by the beginning of the century, the last remaining major obstacle to the legal equality of men and women within marriage, lay in the double standard built into the laws of divorce. This was finally abandoned in 1923 when women were permitted to plead on identical grounds with men, in particular they had to offer no extra grounds other than the adultery of their husbands. In 1925 the conditions for separation and maintenance were further improved, and the 1937 Matrimonial Causes Act (the Herbert Act) which extended the grounds for divorce to include desertion and prolonged insanity, gave equal rights to both sexes. Thus by the middle of this century the only women seriously discriminated against legally were the unmarried mothers. In 1844 the Poor Law Amendment Act had allowed the unmarried mother to lay claims on the biological father to the tune of 2/6 per week, but she could only do this by becoming a charge on the parish. This sum was increased to 5/- in 1872. In 1874 permanent registration in the name of the father was permitted. In 1918 the money was raised to 10/- and in 1923 to £1, and at present it stands at £1 10s.

Thus with the exception of the unmarried mother, the

legal position of the woman today is greatly improved as compared with one hundred years ago, particularly within marriage where the husband has lost the proprietory rights over his wife's person and property, has become liable to proceedings for divorce and the custody of the children, must leave his deserted wife undisturbed in the matrimonial home, and may not exercise the common law right of 'reasonable chastisement' as this is now grounds for divorce. Indeed, the emancipation of married women has led to the creation of a new legal personality—'the married man'.

POLITICAL CHANGES

'. . . The place in which Feminist Movement was born,' said Viola Klein (1949), 'was not the factory nor the mine, but in the Victorian middle-class drawing room.' The problem was one of redundant women, and at the beginning it was essentially a middle-class problem. It is not necessary here to give a detailed analysis of the complex network of causes which gave rise to the revolt of the middle class women, but it is worth noting briefly a few of the more important factors which lay behind the movement.

The first and possibly most important fact was the excess of women over men. The combined effect of a high rate of infant mortality, higher mortality rates generally among men to sickness, emigration, war, and probably, the joys of bachelordom was to create a large class of spinsters. The plight of these spinsters was grave indeed. Lacking education, or the possibility of employment in any sphere save that of governess or seamstress, they faced continual penury during their life with the ever present threat of the workhouse and the disgrace of losing class when they became too old to support themselves. By the end of the century the majority of Victorian families were only too well aware of this problem, as the majority of families contained at least one of these 'surplus' women.

Women had also suffered a decline in economic status as a consequence of the transfer of work out of the home. Whereas before the 'industrial revolution' there was hardly any task that was not performed by women, the transfer of the majority of these tasks from home to factory rapidly led to the view that these tasks were the natural concern of men alone. Middle class women in particular ceased to have an economic value, and were reduced as Mary Wollstonecraft (1792) lamented to the status of birds who were 'confined in their cages' with 'nothing to do but plume themselves and stalk with mock majesty from perch to perch'.

At the same time the concept of 'marital unity' meant that the wife had no legal personality independent from that of her husband. This became more sinister for women, when they found themselves economically utterly dependent on their husbands. Apart from demonstrating the wealth of her husband by her endless leisure, the role of woman was conceived to be one of subservience to her husband, the master and ruler of the family.

The subjection of women in psychological terms went even deeper than the economic and legal facts might suggest. The views of Victorian England as to what constituted the essential 'femaleness' of the female revealed how deeply ideas of her inferiority were taken as part of the natural order of things. As Viola Klein suggested 'the emotional opposition against women's coming of age was gigantic'. Mary Agnes Hamilton (1936) remarked that the general view was that between men and women, there was 'some profound if mysterious difference which, variously as it was described and defined, always somehow disqualified women from citizen action or relevance'. Others such as Gladstone regarded women as superhuman, thus not to be tainted with the ordinary facts of life. Voting for example would he felt 'trespass upon their delicacy, their purity, their refinement, the elevation of their whole nature'.

It is against this background that the movement for the

emancipation of women gathered force. On the one hand it was an act of economic desperation, and on the other it was a claim for identity, political, social, educational and moral, intended as Eleanor Rathbone (1935) said to provide 'a real equality of liberties status and opportunities as between men and women'.

The beginnings of the women's movements were not so much political as economic and educational. 1843 had seen the foundation of the Governesses' Benevolent Institution to provide exams and certificates to governesses, which led to the foundation in 1848 of Queen's College in Harley Street which borrowed its curriculum from the rapidly expanding boys' public schools. The movement for increased education gathered strength as the country as a whole became more conscious of the importance of education. By the end of the century eighty endowed schools for girls had been set up. At the same time despite great opposition the universities had been breached, and between 1869 and 1881 Girton and Newnham were founded at Cambridge and Lady Margaret Hall and Somerville at Oxford, though it was not for some time that they were accorded equal status with the men's colleges. The State system of education which had come into being officially in 1870 provided further opportunities for the education of girls, and the Education Act of 1902 enabled local authorities to maintain and assist secondary schools for both sexes. By 1920 the number of girls receiving secondary education was 185,000, and by 1939 it was over half a million.

Increased educational opportunities meant increased economic opportunities for women, but in the early days progress was only slowly made. In 1859 the Society for the Employment of Women was founded, but for the middle class girl, as Florence Nightingale discovered, it was a long and bitter struggle, and despite the obvious talents of such women as Florence Nightingale, Octavia Hill, Elizabeth Fry, Louisa Twyning or Mary Carpenter, it was not until the Sex Disqualification (Removal) Act of 1919 that the main legal restrictions on women's entry to the professions were cleared away.

Gradually, however, it was on the vote that the energies of the desire for emancipation came to be focused. The first regular suffrage committee was set up in 1855 with Barbara Leigh Smith as Secretary. Its object was to secure the repeal of all laws which discriminated against women, and to obtain complete political equality with men. The idea of female suffrage was first seriously brought up in parliament by John Stuart Mill in May 1867 but was easily defeated. In 1866 The Woman's Suffrage Committee was set up, and for the next forty years the movement, which gained very little interest or publicity from the press, was carried out by the usual methods of meetings, petitions, dissemination of literature and so on. This was the position when the Liberal party achieved power in 1906, having given various assurances of its support for women's suffrage. When it was soon made clear that this support was not genuine, war was declared, and one of the most curious and fascinating movements in the history of this country began —the Militant Suffrage campaign. Mrs. Pankhurst had in fact founded her Women's Social and Political Union in 1905, but it was not really till Sir Henry Campbell Bannerman retired, and Asquith, an avowed opponent of female suffrage, became Prime Minister that hostilities really became violent. Between 1905 and 1909 the main weapons were questions and heckling of Cabinet Ministers at public meetings—often resulting in the ejection of the hecklers with some considerable brutality—deputations to Parliament, and opposition to Government candidates at by-elections. In 1909, window breaking became official policy of Mrs. Pankhurst's Union, and also hunger-striking in prison. The answer to this was the introduction of forcible feeding, and it was the publicity given to this minor form of torture that really threw the campaign into the limelight. Publicity was such that an all party conciliation committee was set up in 1910, which was responsible for the Conciliation Bills of 1910, 1911 and 1912 which each time raised hopes only to have them dashed as the bills failed to get through. Further insult was added in 1911 by the introduction of a male suffrage bill which made absolutely no reference to women. In 1912 frustration reached a new peak and a wide-scale campaign of window smashing took place involving a large number of arrests. A reform bill was promised in April 1913, but failed to get past Mr. Asquith. This led in turn to a campaign of arson; by now forcible feeding was taking its toll of the health of the suffragettes and the famous Cat and Mouse Bill—(Prisoners Temporary Discharge for Ill Health Act) was introduced in 1913, which allowed for the release of prisoners severely debilitated by hunger striking and forcible feeding, and their re-arrest as soon as their health improved. This bill in particular aroused enormous hostility among the suffragettes towards the government. 1913 saw the first and only martyr to the campaign when Emily Davison in June of that year threw herself under the King's horse during the Derby. Public opinion had begun to swing towards the campaign, and the movement itself had widened its base by Sylvia Pankhurst's work in the East End among working class women. But in 1914 came the outbreak of war, and militancy ceased, amnesty was granted to all suffrage prisoners, and women went to work for 'King and Country'.

There will probably be no final answer as to whether the campaign would have achieved its goal so quickly had there been no war. Certainly the war, as did the second world war, played an enormous part in breaking down the most rigid divisions between what constituted male activity and what constituted female. Also the end of the war—as again in 1945—represented a time of hope and of idealism when social reform was a welcome outlet for such feelings.

In 1918 a bill was passed giving the vote to all men over twenty-one and women over thirty. Complete equality was granted in 1928, but there was no dancing in the streets, no massive celebration. The original enthusiasms of the campaign had been spent. The terrible loss of men killed in the war, the war widows, and the onset of mass unemployment created quite a new post-war climate of other problems, while the brightest of the new younger generation were busy dancing and flirting their way through the Jazz age. The early suffragettes of which Mrs. Pankhurst was a prime example had been forced by the circumstances either to deny their femininity and pretend to be male, or to vaunt their female state as superior to that of men. The bright young things of the nineteen-twenties wanted none of this; so the movement petered out. The vote had been won, and if the problems for which the vote had been the symbolic solution, had not been entirely resolved, no one seemed to care very much.

Chapter Two

GENERAL CHANGES IN THE STRUCTURE AND PATTERNS OF FAMILY LIFE

IF the legal, economic, political and educational changes that have affected women in the past one hundred years constitute a social revolution, it must not be forgotten that changes within the family have also taken place within the last one hundred years, which constitute a revolution in themselves, and have fundamentally altered the life pattern of women. Some of the most important of these changes are demographic.

The fall in the birth rate which began in the 1870's has provided one of the most fascinating puzzles for demographers and sociologists alike. The best analysis of this development, which has occurred in the majority of industrialised countries is still probably *Prosperity and Parenthood* (Banks, 1954). The decline in the birth rate in this country began in the 1870's among the middle classes representing what might be called a retreat from parenthood and from a rate of 35·4 per thousand it fell steadily to 14 per thousand at the end of the thirties. The beginning of this decline which meant a fundamental reduction in family size came at a time when the real Victorian boom was over. Standards of living had been raised during that period, as had been aspirations and no one wished to give up their newly won prosperity. Between 1850–70 prices rose by 5%, and by 1870 Banks estimates the average family had increased its outlay by

50%. With the spread of compulsory education children had ceased to be economic assets, while at the same time opportunities for children to advance were legion, and middle class parents were quick to see this. The first stirrings of the Women's Movement had begun by 1870 and women had begun to question everything about their lives including incessant child bearing. Annie Besant's birth control movement came in for a good deal of publicity during the trial of 1877, and between then and 1921 over three million pamphlets were circulated.

Whereas women born between 1841 and 1845 were producing average familes of 5·71 children, women born between 1900 and 1909 had familes of 3·37 children. For those born between 1925 and 1929 the figure was 2·19. At the beginning of this century, the fall in the birth rate spread to the working classes, and the differential between manual and non-manual families fell from 1·15 for those married between 1900 and 1909 to ·76 for 1925–9 marriages. By 1924 the largest average families (3·35) were among the unskilled labourers, and the smallest (1·65) among the salaried employees. The birth rate rose sharply after the war, then settled, as it appeared, at about 15·6 per thousand (1956). However, very recently the rate has risen again to around 17 per thousand live births, which may indicate an increase in family size among the middle classes. However, as compared to the size among the middle of the last century, and the number of pregnancies involved to produce such large familes, there is no denying the total change in the life pattern of married women. Studies in birth control such as that by Rowntree and Pierce (1961) reveal a steady increase in its use among all classes, and an increase in its use from the onset of marriage. At the beginning of this century the average woman could expect to spend one-third of her life producing children. Today the figure is nearer to one-fifteenth.

During the latter half of the nineteenth century and the beginning of this century marriage rates among women were declining probably through a combination of Victorian prudence, lack of men, and new found ideas of independence. However, one of the striking demographic facts of the last forty years has been the rapid and increasing popularity of marriage. Between 1911 and 1947 the proportion of women aged between 20 and 24 who were married rose steadily. The trend has been continued up to the present time. This is reflected in the falling age of marriage. In 1960 9% of all grooms were under 21 and 36·4% of all brides were under 21. Both these figures represented an increase over the recent past.

These are the key demographic changes of the past one hundred years which have revolutionised the life of women, from one of constant child-bearing, ill health, and early loss of youth to a life in which ten years at most are devoted to the production and care of small children.

One of the factors which has vitally affected the role of women within the family is the relationship between the nuclear family and its wider circle of kin. Writers on the sociology of the family have, in the main, tended to see two basic family types, the one based on tradition and the extended family, the other temporary and isolated justified solely by the marriage bond. Carstairs (1964) in his Reith lectures laid great stress on the isolation of the nuclear family, which he said provided a seed bed for many of the troubles and difficulties that we face today. At the same time British sociologists have indicated the existence of a widespread network of extended families. These were originally considered to be remnants of 'old' systems surviving in pockets of the past, such as Bethnal Green or Ship Street. However, extended family systems were also found in places that were well connected with twentieth century life, such as Woodford or Dagenham. In the United States, studies also showed that among middle class families extended relationships are the norm. Against all this is the evidence of Peter Laslett (1963), which indicates that family size in the seventeenth century was very similar to that of our own time. 'If we do not find ourselves in large families of several generations living together, or in joint families containing lots of relatives no more did they.' In fact the explanation for this probably lies in the confusing of two separate trends. On the one hand we have unmistakable evidence of the existence of the extended family in our society, not quite in the form practised by the middle class families of the nineteenth century, but more as an agency of mutual aid and as a continual source of social intercourse. Among the working classes this type of family life, which probably had no opportunity to exist until the beginning of this century, developed in areas of relative stability to provide a bulwark against depression and poverty. The advantages to its members proved such that despite housing schemes, general mobility, and slum clearance, it is still practised in some form by the majority of families.

At the same time the increased recognition of the importance of the individual has had its effects, not so much on the structure of family life, but on the ideology which surrounds it. For the modern family is expected to give much more recognition to the individual than was the case in the past. (This shift from group functioning to individual function has proved a problem to many Africans who come to the towns to find to their surprise that whole families cannot find work as a group—they had never thought of themselves as anything but a unit.) Thus though the majority of people today live within some type of extended family system, the stress placed on the importance of the individual makes this appear more to be a matter of personal choice than of outside pressures. In fact as Peter Laslett says the incidence of isolation, broken homes, and so on was probably worse three hundred years ago. What *is* specifically different is that we live longer, we know far more, we move freely and are more clearly individuals. What is important for this study is that extended family or no, the tyranny of the Victorian family over its members in general, and the women in particular has undoubtedly declined. 'The

Family today,' says O. R. McGregor (1960), 'is the product on the one hand of the diffusion of the democratic habit and the destruction of Victorian domestic tyrannies. . . .' The tyrant was the male head of the family supported by an ideology of family life which encouraged subservience amongst its female members. In the average family life as it is lived today the worth of every individual member, and that includes the female members, is not questioned.

If women as women have gained freedom through the democratisation of family life, they have also gained freedom as children, and as adolescents. Until the last century, parental rights over their children were as absolute as those of any monarch, and until the nineteenth century there was no statutory law in existence concerned with children. In the early stages of the nineteenth century the improvement of the position of the child in law was merely part of the improvement in the position of women, that is the gradual extension of the mother's rights over her child as compared to that of the father. Not till 1889 was an Act passed that acknowledged the right of the child to be protected from the parents. This Act made parents legally obliged to maintain their children in a proper condition and health, and failure to do this could involve loss of parental rights. Today, of course, the child is considered to have a full legal, social and psychological value independent of his parents. Indeed as far as psychological pressures are concerned the tables may be said to have turned, and it is the parent who is put second to the child. Certainly the development of psychological theories in the post-Freudian era, and more recently the widespread dissemination of theories of maternal deprivation have all served to give the child a value as great if not greater than that of parents. So far this development has seen no serious differentiation made between the female and the male child. The delicate mechanisms that go to make up the human personality, which are so vulnerable in the early stages apply to male and female alike, and the female child has been freed from the absolute tyranny of her father in the same way that she has as an adult been liberated from the tyranny of her mate.

The role of the adolescent in modern society and his or her relationship with her family has been for some time a subject of continuing interest. As T. R. Fyvel (1961) said 'As the first half of this century has seen the . . . emancipation of women, so the second half may see a parallel emancipation of adolescents.' Certainly the existence of a 'youth culture' is without dispute. Essentially working class, and exploited commercially, it is symbolised by the Pop songs (which today are not the province of the working class alone) catering for what *Time* magazine once called 'Teen feel', in which the illusions of youth are exalted as being the only things of value in a dark and oppressive world. The independence of modern adolescents has been noted in practically every European country since the war, even in Russia. Certainly one of the important facts about the modern teenager is his increased earning power, both compared to teenagers before the war, and as compared to his own parents. According to Mark Abrams (1961) 'real earnings of teenagers have risen much faster than those of adults . . .' The analysis by Abrams of how teenagers spent their money (and in 1959 he estimated it to be in total £830 millions in Great Britain) reveals the most clear cut pattern of tastes specifically directed at those ends which form part of the youth culture. Teenage expenditure formed at least 25% of all expenditure on motor cycles, records and record players, cosmetics and on the cinema. The average boy spent a pound a week on drinks, cigarettes and entertainment, the average girl spent a pound a week on clothes, cosmetics and shoes. So the adolescent girl in the brief period between childhood and marriage has been released from her dependence on her family, both by her potential earning power, and by her ability to pass into a world of her own, dominated by her peers which may appear totally alien to her parents.

No discussion on changing family patterns in Britain can conclude without making specific mention of working class family life. When Booth made his survey of London at the end of the last century he found evidence of much instability in family life. The incidence of drinking was high, partly due to the 'intolerable discomfort of the home', which sent men, women and children out to seek comfort elsewhere, and witnesses complained that 'instead of cooking, women stand gossiping all morning and then send out to the ham and beef shop'.

In fact, as Roger Wilson (1963) has suggested, over the last one hundred and fifty years, the pattern of working class life has changed three times. In the early period of industrialism the working classes became unsuccessful urban dwellers. 'In this unfamiliar world the best were at sea, the worst cut off their immediate perplexities by drink— drunk for 1d., dead drunk for 2d.' Gradually, roots were put down, economic conditions improved, and there came in this century a growth of stability and communal life. This trend of life has been described by David Lockwood (1960) as 'a social universe in which the same sort of people work and live in close relationship with one another strongly under the sway of a group ethos which places a premium on immediate rather than distant goals . . .' The home was overcrowded and unattractive, and the pub and the working man's club were places of refuge and escape. This too was the world of 'Mum', who emerged as the dominant character. Just as in pre-industrial times father and son had been linked by their common property rights and common occupation, and the handing down of a skill or craft, so the Mother stood out as the one source of stability, inheriting her occupation from her mother, passing on what skills she possessed to her daughter. 'The extended family,' suggested Young and Willmott, was the woman's trade union— 'Organised by women for women'. Life for women in these circumstances was not solely joy and cosiness as some current popular sociology or literature might suggest.

Letters from working wives to the Co-operative Women's
Guild in 1915 speak of misery, pain and ill health—'I am a
ruined woman through having children,' wrote one. 'There
is certainly no rest for mothers night or day,' said another.
Mrs. Pember Reeves writing in 1913 discussed the difficulties of the *Poor and Marriage*. The chief worry, she felt
was that 'there is to be still another baby with the inevitable
consequences—more crowding, more illness, more worry,
more work and less food, less strength, less time to manage
with'. In *The Woman in the Little House*, M. L. Eyles (1922)
found sex to be a constant problem—summed up by the
remark, 'I shouldn't mind about married life so much if it
wasn't for bedtime'. Sexual intercourse was regarded by
men as 'their rights' and the reluctance of the wife to co-
operate was viewed with injured hostility. The picture
presented by Margery Spring-Rice (1939) in her *Working
Class Wives* is hardly more cheerful. She found the majority
on an insufficient diet, sacrificing themselves for the sake of
their husbands and children, overworked, spending most of
the day on their feet with no rest—'our husbands do not
realise that we ever need any leisure'. She concluded that the
lives of these women were an unremitting picture of 'mono-
tony, loneliness, discouragement and sordid hard work.'

However, not all the working class lived under such
conditions; even before the war, large sections of the working class who had found their way into the expanding light
industries experienced a fair degree of prosperity. Never-
theless for the working class as a whole, the movement into
Roger Wilson's third stage—dominated by mobility, increased consumption and mass cultural intake—came only
after the war with continued full employment and the consumption boom of the fifties. Only in the last twenty years
has the working class home really become a place that is
warm, comfortable, able to provide its own fireside entertainment.

This has not meant as some suggest the *embourgeoise-
ment* of working class life, for as Peter Laslett (1961) says

'to call the prosperous working class family of the nineteen sixties bourgeois or middle class is a superficial historical misconception. It is merely the working class family of the nineteen hundreds, of the nineteen twenties or of the nineteen thirties with the horror of poverty removed.'

Nor has the increased material prosperity among large (but by no means all) sectors of the working class brought with it an automatic assumption of what many people feel to be middle class norms—thrift, delaying of goals, ambition, the desire for respectability and withdrawal from neighbourly contacts. As Bennet Berger (1960) argues, 'Middle class symbols have so long been identified with the enemies of the labour movement, socialism and the working class, that relatively high standards of living may tend to be perceived as evidence of the disappearance of a real working class, instead of as *conditions* capable of generating a consciousness of collective achievement which is worth fighting to preserve.'

Chapter Three

THE FAMILY TODAY

TO complete this summary of changes affecting the family in this country, we must consider the family today. In demographic terms, it can be said that the average marriage produces two to three children as compared to numbers in excess of six one hundred and fifty years ago. On the other hand the expectation of life of its members is now at least seventy which means that every family has to face the problem of how to care for the very old. It is no longer dominated (demographically) by women, as the reduced infant mortality rates ensure that the majority of male off-spring survive. The increased popularity of marriage at ever earlier ages means that the conjugal family spends the greater proportion of its time as a unit of two. The family is also supported in a great many ways by the State today, which was not true in the nineteenth century. Health, education, and to some degree housing, are the concern of the State. Compulsory insurance provides some protection against misfortune, and the tax system is geared to favour the family as against the single. It should not, however, be thought that this support to the family has been at great cost to the nation. There is no evidence to support the view that 'the admitted and always approved benefits of greater material security have been purchased at the price of a steady weakening in the structure of society'. This support is a necessary concomitant of an industrial society which both reduces the power of the family to be a self-contained unit, and demands of it extremely high standards of care for its members. As McGregor (1960) suggests, 'Nineteenth cen-

22

tury industrialism created an urban society in which only affluent families could self-helpfully discharge their functions and responsibilities.'

Some critics of the modern Family have argued that these 'functions and responsibilities' have been considerably reduced in the period since industrialisation. The modern family, says MacIver and Page (1949), has been stripped of all non-essential functions and its role today is simply to harmonise three major functions, namely the satisfaction of sexual needs, the procreation and rearing of children, and the provision of a home. Talcott Parsons (1955) suggests that in a 'highly differentiated society' the functions of the family 'are not to be interpreted as functions directly on behalf of society, but on behalf of personality'. The two basic functions of the family are therefore: (1) the primary socialisation of the children, and (2) the stabilisation of the adult personalities of the population of the society. This accords with the view of Bryan Wilson (1962) who argued that the family has simply become a 'highly specialised agency for affection'. However, to present the family's functions in so limited a way is both to misunderstand the past and misrepresent the present. As Nels Anderson (1960) suggests, 'the idea seems to be current that if the family changes it can only be for the worse, and that such change endangers society'. Indeed the family has changed as has society, in the past one hundred and fifty years, but the general direction of that change has been towards increasing complexity of function rather than the reverse. Thus as Ronald Fletcher (1962) says, 'the family is now concerned with a more detailed and refined satisfaction of needs than hitherto, and it is also more intimately and responsibly bound up with the wider and more complicated network of social institutions in the modern state than it was prior to industrialism'. As far as the essential functions described by MacIver are concerned—sexual, procreative, and the provision of a home, higher standards are demanded by society today than ever they were in the nineteenth century. Parenthood and the care of children is now a highly self-conscious affair in which the maintenance of a high standard is insisted upon, and the pitfalls are for ever being exposed. The importance of the home today is underlined continually by the mass media particularly through advertisements, the house in particular is usually shown as being well stocked with appliances and comforts, clean, bright and up to date. The revolution of rising expectations ensures that the desire to improve one's home is one of the constant pre-occupations of the family. As far as the satisfaction of the sexual needs is concerned higher standards are asked of the family than ever before, particularly as fertility is now susceptible to control. The concept of romantic love drawing its inspiration largely from legends about knights and ladies is still with us, and is reinforced by the pop song, the advertisement, the magazine, which never cease to extol the virtues of love as a solution to all problems and as a basis for all thought. In a society in which divorce is tolerated if not approved, marriages are expected to provide positive advantages to the partners in order that they continue to stay together. If the family's essential functions are possibly more complex than in previous times, it has also acquired more functions. Economically the family functions as a unit of consumption, as a provider and improver of homes, as a possessor and maintainer of property. As far as education is concerned the extension of State and private provisions has by no means served to reduce the functions of the family in this sphere. The demands of a complex industrial society are such that education is the keystone to adult success. The family must prepare the child in its early years in such a way that it is ready to receive an education and receptive to it. Throughout his attendance at school the child will need support, assistance and direction from his parents, particularly when he nears the end, and a multiplicity of choices are available upon which his future may depend. Just how important this can be has been revealed by recent studies of the working class and education, which demonstrate to what extent working class children are handicapped by their family's lack of understanding of the education system, and their inability or unwillingness to support their children emotionally and intellectually throughout their school career. As is the case with publicly provided education, Fletcher suggests the wider health services have by no means taken over all the functions which previously were performed by the family. The family is still the prime guardian of its members' health, and the standards demanded of it are now incomparably greater than they were even fifty years ago. To these functions, now extended, must be added recreation, something that was until recently purely a province of the upper classes. The 'weekend' is now a time of leisure and family activity which is only partially provided for by television and the growth of the entertainment industry.

In fact, says Fletcher, the main functions of the family in our society can be summarised as follows:

1. It provides a way of regulating sexual behaviour.
2. It gives a legitimate basis for the procreation and rearing of children.
3. Provides sustenance and care for its dependent members.
4. It is of primary importance as an agency of socialisation and of education, and thus of the transmission of culture.
5. It bestows titles, roles and duties on its members which are recognised and applied by society (son, husband, wife, etc.).

The next point to consider in any analysis of the modern family is the question—is it inherently unstable? Once again there are many people both sociologists and laymen who are convinced that it is. Sociologists such as Zimmerman (1947) or MacIver, who have seen the history of the family as a succession of types, have all tended to regard the modern family in rather a pessimistic light. The detailed arguments of those who feel the family today to be unstable, with specific reference to Great Britain, rest largely on the following assumptions:

1. The family today is an isolated unit unable and unwilling to seek assistance in its distress from wider circles of kin (as it has always done in the past).
2. There has been a loss of authority—primarily moral within the family giving rise to ever increasing delinquency.
3. Sexual morality is at a low ebb and is continuing to decline as evidenced in the increase in venereal disease, illegitimacy and divorce.
4. That family life has been seriously endangered by the increase in married women working who thereby neglect and abandon their children and husbands, creating a host of problems as a result.
5. That its role in society has been undermined by the Welfare State.

As has been demonstrated above, the functions of the family have been extended in this century rather than curtailed. Basically many of those who argue that the contemporary family is unstable, have in their minds the Victorian middle class family as an ideal norm from which we have strayed. This is conceived of as a perfect example of authority, stability and moral rectitude which provided a linch-pin for a virtuous, stable and moral society. Compared with this ideal, the modern family has suffered a loss of parental authority. This, however, is of course extremely difficult to analyse because in such matters there is always a gap between ideal and reality. Certainly the Victorian father was accorded more authority by society than his equivalent today, but there are few who would today argue in favour of the complete dictatorship of such a father, and a great deal of the legislation in the last one hundred and fifty years has been directed quite deliberately at reducing this authority and giving equal status to the women and children. In a more subtle form, however, it could be argued that there has been not so much a loss of authority as a loss of contact between parents and their adolescent children, which may well be *one* of the factors contributing to the undoubted increase in delinquency in all such

societies as our own. But the blame cannot be laid specifically at the family's door; the problem of delinquency
involves the whole of the society we live in, its material and
psychological attributes, its ideals and its ability to live up
to them. Thus while it might be fair to argue that rising
delinquency rates are signs of strain within the Family,
they are not conclusive evidence of its increasing instability.
Much the same arguments can be advanced on the subject
of sexual morality. Increasing divorce rates must be seen
against increasing marriage rates, and a falling average age
of marriage. Two world wars this century have produced
great social confusion from which we have slowly re-
covered. What is more, as Rowntree and Carrier (1958)
point out, divorce rates are to some extent a product of the
legal provisions in existence. It is also worth noting that
Rowntree and Carrier found that marriages contracted
since 1945 show some signs of being more stable than
those contracted in the previous twenty years. Increasing
illegitimacy rates may in part reflect the disorientation of
the young, though as previously mentioned this is not
totally the fault of an unstable family, it also reflects the
ambivalence in our society towards sexual behaviour, with
a widening degree of permissiveness in private, while in
public the Victorian attitudes remain. It also may be a
result of the rise in status of women, who no longer feel
impelled to treasure their virginity and thus feel freer to
enter into pre-marital sexual relationships.

The controversy over women working will be discussed
in detail at a later stage. As far as the stability of the family
is concerned there is little indication of serious neglect,
and it is certain that many *working* class children get far
more parental care today than they did one hundred years
ago. The typical working wife is in fact not the mother of
young children, but is likely to be aged between forty and
fifty with most if not all her children grown up. Studies
such as those by Yudkin and Holme (1965) reveal no
evidence of severe damage to children, and these studies

revealed, as did Viola Klein's (1958) that the majority of working wives have the support and approval of their husbands. Once again there is little evidence here to support the view that the family is unstable and in decline.

What is true is that the family today gives much more recognition to the individual as a self sufficient independent person. Increased mobility and the decline of hereditary privilege have combined to reduce the power of the family to confer status and increase the responsibility of the individual to find at least in part his own level, through achievement rather than ascription. Family relationships today may be less dependent on outside pressure and more dependent on their own internal structure. But this does not imply that they are any less strong. It must also be remembered that the quality of family life today is considered a matter of public concern, sufficiently so the State and society at large, feels entitled to look in, and complain or take action if necessary. In a sense we are subjecting family life to a detailed factual scrutiny which would have been unthinkable, for example, to the Victorians. Obviously the result of such vigilance is to reveal the faults. But because we did not look before we cannot assume that these faults were not there. However, it does seem that the modern family, as a social institution, stands reasonably clear and firm today, approved of by its members (as rising marriage rates, falling age of marriages and a rising birth rate attest) and supported by the State through a network of financial and social services.

Before, however, leaving the contemporary family one last point needs briefly to be mentioned although it will be discussed in detail during the survey. This is the question as to what extent can we speak of 'the family' in England today instead of the 'working class families' and 'middle class families'. 'A century ago,' said McGregor and Rowntree (1962), 'middle and working class families shared little in common save their high fertilities.' In the twentieth century they suggest 'the reduction in family size and the extensions of social policy have together given working people the means to adopt some habits of middle class life'.

In fact many differences still remain; studies such as those by the Institute of Community Studies reveal some sections of working class family life to be everywhere more family and neighbourhood bound than in the middle class. The importance of 'Mum' continues to be in its most extreme form a working class phenomenon. Studies of child rearing such as that by the Newsons (1963) indicate sharp differences in patterns of behaviour. What is more, evidence provided by the Newsons, Zweig (1961) and this study indicate that while the old working class family may have sharply divided into male and female, amongst the young there is more sharing of domesticity amongst the working class than in the middle. Culturally, as revealed by educational success, and choices of leisure and entertainment, there is a gap between working and middle class taste which is only occasionally bridged. What is more, increased material prosperity among certain sections of the working class has not automatically been followed by the adoption of middle class patterns.

Indeed one of the points that this survey will highlight is the continuing differences in working class patterns of family life as compared to middle class, although our interest will be chiefly focused on those differences which affect the relative roles of women.

Chapter Four

CHANGING PATTERNS OF WORK

AT the beginning of this decade approximately six million women were working. Over half of them were married women. At the beginning of this century only about one-quarter of the women who worked were married. In considering some of the factors that lie behind this change, it should first be remembered that with the exception of the middle classes in the nineteenth century, women have always worked, and until the growth of the factory system activities such as weaving, making clothes, baking, preserving, were all the special province of women.

It was only when work left the home, that the dual pull of home versus work became the reality it is today. In the early part of the nineteenth century the middle class wife opted for home and the working class wife took her Hobson's choice and worked alongside her children to create what Myrdal and Klein (1956) call 'one of the blackest spots in the social history of the nineteenth century'. By the second half of the century, the middle class wife was beginning to strain at the leash, while the working class wife had had some restrictions placed upon her employment for her own protection. However, even among middle class wives there was no great enthusiasm for a dual role. Their concern was more for those who were destined not to marry, and many of the early feminists consciously denied their femininity to assert their independence. Others exalted it, but all agreed that men were a brake rather than an asset to women's ambitions.

At the turn of the century 25% of all employable women

were out at work but the vast majority were unmarried girls under thirty-five. 90% of all women clerks were single, and 75% of all female operatives in spinning and weaving were also single. In fact the majority of women left paid employment when they married and so saw their life as having two phases. Firstly they left school and went out to work; and secondly they got married and stopped working. Employers saw their female labour force conditioned by the expectation of marriage and they accepted and expected a high turnover, took advantage of the speed and dexterity of the young to channel them into semi-skilled and repetitive work. There was an understandable reluctance to train women for skilled work.

What has happened in the sixty years of this century has been a fundamental change in the structure of the female working population, from single to married, from young to middle aged. As Le Gros Clark (1963) says, 'The typical working woman of today is no longer the immature and pliable girl, who was so demonstrably filling in time until she got married; the typical working woman tends on the contrary to be a married woman in her middle life.' In this sense the problem of the working wife and mother is of fairly recent origin. Women, as Myrdal and Klein point out, had been 'squeezed out of the economic process' by the industrial revolution. The first stage of their return was led by the unmarried, and only recently has the married woman attempted to combine home and work simultaneously.

Certainly one vital factor which has assisted in the creation of this change has been the reduction in family size. Today the majority of families are completed within ten years of marriage. Add to this the fact that marriages are beginning at an earlier age, and it is fair to estimate that most mothers will have borne their last child by the age of thirty. General improvements in mortality rate, accentuated for women by a decrease in the hazards of child-bearing, have meant that the average woman has half a century or more ahead of her at her marriage. Even if she delays her children and waits until the youngest is an adolescent before considering herself a possible candidate for work she is unlikely to be more than forty-five and has thus at least fifteen years of working life ahead. Clearly more married women are able to go to work today because they have a much greater degree of freedom from family life.

A second important demographic factor is the increased popularity of marriage, coupled with falling age rates for marriage. This combined with the excess of males in the marriageable age groups has meant that the problem of the 'redundant women' which so troubled the Victorians is a thing of the past and the spinster is rapidly becoming a rarity. Thus in simple terms of addition and subtraction the proportion of women working who are married must rise, as it has done, and the numbers of the single decline. In fact Viola Klein (1965) in her latest study estimates that by 1973 there will be nine million women working in Britain of whom over 60% will be married.

The two world wars have also had a great impact on the patterns of work, creating as it were an emergency situation in which all available labour was made use of, and demarcation lines between what was considered male and female work had to be abandoned. The First World War saw the first wide scale employment of women in the manufacturing industry, and their introduction to skilled work, although in the Lancashire cotton industry it had been traditional for many years to employ married women in skilled work. In the inter-war period the widespread unemployment reduced the availability of work all round, but the Second World War saw a mobilisation of the country's labour resources on an even wider scale than in 1914. As Pearl Jephcott (1962) pointed out, 'Company rules and customs which had prevented the employment of married women were abandoned, and as the war developed and the labour shortage became more acute a variety of special part-time shifts and other concessions were introduced to facilitate the employment of women with domestic responsibilities.' With continued full employment after the war, managements had no alternative but to continue to offer employment to married women even if they regarded it as a temporary expedient.

The growth of mass production and its breakdown of skilled work into repetitive semi-skilled or unskilled work opened up new possibilities for employment for women. In factory employment women have probably been the beneficiaries of the machine. The growth of new industries unhampered by traditions that the nature of the work involved is more suited to men, such as the consumption industries, have offered further opportunities for women, their attraction for employers being in the main the fact that they could be paid less. The growth of commerce and administration has been an important factor in increasing women's work, and at the higher level the expansion of the teaching, nursing and social services has provided a whole range of occupations for educated women. The great expansion of the service industries such as cleaning, retail distribution and catering has also provided employment for women directly related to their experience at home and has proved an attraction to women who might in earlier times have gone into domestic service. In short as Pearl Jephcott says, 'more married women are able to go out to work for three major reasons—because there are more jobs available, because there are fewer single women to fill them, and because reduced family responsibilities and a longer life allow the wife and mother to commit herself to work outside the home'.

The pattern today is work until marriage, work after marriage until the children arrive, and a return to work when the children grow older. Thus marriage and a family no longer mean an end to paid employment for women, but simply an interruption.

Chapter Five

A SUMMARY

TO summarise, very briefly, what has been discussed and to bring the picture up to date, we can say that:

1. Legally and politically women apart from one or two minor points are equal to men.
2. Demographically the one-time surplus has now become a shortage and women of marriageable age are now outnumbered by men.
3. Their period as wives is increasing as the age of marriage falls and the expectation of life increases.
4. Their period as active mothers has decreased as family size has fallen and child-bearing has been compressed into a short period following upon marriage.
5. In educational terms opportunities are not far short of those provided for men.
6. Opportunities for work have greatly increased, particularly in some of the newer industries.
7. The working class woman has benefited very greatly from the general rise in standards of living.

If all these changes are considered together, then three major developments can be noted which have particular relevance to this study:

1. The status of women in relation to men has risen considerably.
2. The number of roles which women can perform in society has increased and become more varied.
3. Women have experienced an extension in the freedom of choice as to which roles they wish to perform.

Yet in 1956 the *Economist* published an article entitled 'The

Feminists Mop Up' in which it was said, 'More than a century after Florence Nightingale staged her passionate revolt against the trivial domestic round here are the mass of women still preoccupied with their love life, clothes, children and homes—all the stuff of the women's magazines . . . The ordinary woman persists in the belief that in marriage one ounce of perfume is still worth a peck of legal rights and her dreams of power still feature the *femme fatale* rather than the administrative grade of the Civil Service. The working class woman especially is almost untouched by the women's movements.'

Can this be true? Have all the great changes in the position of women in the last one hundred and fifty years come to nothing? The only way to begin to answer this is to study women themselves, in detail, because it is the details which added together will reveal something of the nature and quality of the lives being led by women today.

PART TWO

The Survey

Chapter Six

BACKGROUND OF THE SAMPLES[1]

AS has been said, the aim of this study was to concentrate on young married women, and the average age of the forty-eight women in the working class sample was twenty-five (at the time of interview), the median age was twenty-five, and the ages ranged from nineteen to thirty-one.

The working classes are traditionally area bound, and even here where there is a fairly high turnover of population, 35% of the women in the sample were born in the area—that is in the borough of St. Pancras. 79% of the sample were Londoners, and were thus living in the city of their birth. 75% of the wives' parents were also Londoners by birth, 10% having been born locally. Of those parents who were still living, 71% were now living in London as well.

Changes in Family Size

A change in family size might be indicated by comparing the size of family from which these women came with the size of family they planned for themselves. 37% came from families of six children or more. Only 2% planned to have six children. 45% of the women came from families of four children or more, yet only 23% planned themselves to have four or more. 50% intended to have no more than two children; 4% of the mothers wanted one child only. Despite the present rise in the birth rate, which these families in fact just precede, as compared with their own parents they show a clear decline in family size.

[1] The samples both number 48.

Memories of Childhood

Memories of childhood vary, both in their accuracy as to the way the individual felt at the time, and to their truthfulness. However everyone was asked whether they felt they had had a happy childhood. Despite the ambiguity of the word happy no one appeared to have the slightest difficulty in answering this question, and analysis of the replies reveal 48% of the wives considered they had had an unhappy childhood.

'It was rows, rows, rows,' said a bench-fitter's wife, 'that's all I remember, rows with me, rows between Mum and Dad, it never stopped.' 'It wasn't too good,' said the wife of a bus driver. 'Dad left us when I was six, we were better off without him, he was very violent, then my Mam had to work very hard. She was a good mother but even so. . . .' Another bad father was reported by a sheet metal worker's wife, 'My Mam was wonderful—but Dad—I think he was mad, he would knock us around, in fact I left home when I was seventeen because he beat me when I lent a book to an Italian friend. He said I shouldn't lend books to foreigners.'

6% of the wives had been brought up by foster parents and had not been at all happy. One wife married to a dress cutter complained bitterly: 'My foster parents just didn't understand children, and the husband, well he was under his wife's thumb. I got away just as soon as I could and came back to my real Mum.' Those who felt theirs had been a happy childhood were equally emphatic. 'We were a real happy family,' was one comment. 'Admittedly Dad worked long hours so we didn't see too much of him. But my Mum . . . well you wouldn't believe it but I never went anywhere without her. I even used to take her with me on a Saturday night!' 'They were very strict,' said a printer's wife, who came from a family of eleven, 'but we had everything we ever wanted.' 'We couldn't have been happier,' said a gardener's wife, 'though I couldn't exactly tell you why.'

48% of those whose childhood memories had not been pleasant ones felt that their relationships with at least one if not both parents were now reasonably amicable. But the others, 52%, considered that the unhappy relationships of childhood had persisted into adult life, and despite the release of tension through living away from home, relations between them and their parents continued to be bad. As the wife of a foreman put it, 'We simply don't get on, I must have the last word, and so must they—well you can guess the result.'

Education
Despite the fact that half the sample came from a background of skilled manual workers or small shopowners, only 20% of the wives went to grammar schools, and 73% left school at fifteen. This exodus confirms the point made in the Crowther Report (1960) that 'among the families of manual workers it is still the exception for a child to stay at school after he is legally free to go.' For girls this may reflect the lure of adult life, and the desire to wear the latest clothes, and enjoy the brief 'golden' period between school and marriage. As J. B. Mays (1962) says, 'Young people's ambitions are limited, their economic goals short term, and bound up with immediate cash returns, and this attitude tends to reduce the appeal of education.'

Husband's Background
The average age of the husbands in the sample was twenty-nine, though the ages ranged from twenty-one to forty-one. As in the case of their wives, the great majority were Londoners and 35% were born in the area. 56% of the husband's parents were also Londoners by birth, and again as in the case of their wives, only a very few were now living outside London. There were in fact four families in which both husband and wife and all four parents had been born in the locality. In 23% of cases, both sets of parents were living close by.

Memories of Childhood

No first hand information could be obtained on this subject, and the husbands were rarely present at the interviews. However, the respondents were asked to describe as best they could how their husbands felt about their childhoods. Despite mixed feelings about their parents-in-law, which in some cases the wives were unable to hide—(a 'coalie's' wife said, 'Him and his family, I got a positive thing about it, they are so close.')—65% concluded that their husband's childhood had been happy. But the greater degree of unhappiness was recollected by the wives about their own childhood which accords with the findings of D. Pond, A. Ryle and M. Hamilton (1963) who found that a larger number of women reported disturbed childhoods than men. The explanation for this, and indeed for the higher rates of neurosis among women of all ages is as yet not clear. However in terms of childhood experience it certainly could be argued that the nature of the role of a girl in the family is such as to make her more exposed to family disturbances than that of a boy.

Education

As with their wives, only a small number of husbands went to grammar school, 23%, and 75% left school at fifteen or earlier. However, despite the exodus from school, 64% were now in occupations which were either skilled or 'white collar' and incomes varied from seven to thirty pounds a week. (6% of the wives did not know what their husbands earned, and 2% firmly refused to say what was the amount.) The average wage of those who gave the information was between £13/10/– and £14/10/– per week.

If we summarise from this, then it can be said that the typical working class wife in this survey was born in London, as were her parents, and her husband was born in London as well. Both she and her husband went to secondary modern schools and left by fifteen. Her childhood was more likely to have been unhappy than that of her husband, but, now that she is married, and away from home, relations with both sets of parents are likely to be amicable at worst, very close at best. The typical wife is aged about twenty-five, her husband a few years older, and he is employed in some skilled or semi-skilled capacity earning around fourteen pounds per week.

2. MIDDLE CLASS

If we turn now to the middle class sample, certain differences immediately become apparent. Firstly the middle class wives were slightly older. The average age was twenty-seven, and the youngest was twenty-three, so there were no teenage wives in the middle class group.

The middle classes are, as is known, not so area-bound as the working classes, and there was no one in the group who was living in the same district as the one in which she had been born. 25% of the sample were Londoners by birth, and 5% of these had parents who were also Londoners. 17% of the wives had at least one parent who had been born abroad, the countries varying from India to Germany.

Families of origin were smaller than those of the working class. 83% came from families averaging three children or less, and only 4% came from families of six or more. In fact there is some evidence that the intentions of these wives in terms of their own family size show a slight increase on the previous generation. 12% of the wives had no brothers or sisters, yet one mother alone planned to have only one child, and she had some doubts about this. 25% of the wives were planning to have at least four children, yet only 17% came from families of this size.

Memories of Childhood
Middle class girls appeared more critical of their past than the working class, 15% of the wives felt their childhoods had been very unhappy. Evacuation had been a problem for

43

some. ' I had a happy beginning,' said the wife of a sales manager, 'but at four I was evacuated for six years. They were not nice people and I can still remember how unhappy I was.' The wife of a teacher was evacuated to 'a maiden aunt' and she 'was very strict and there was too much Church.' 'I was sent to America. I was unhappy and I found it very confusing having two lots of parents,' said the wife of an actor. Another teacher's wife suffered from having a mother who believed in emancipation and felt herself to be unemancipated. 'My mother was an ex-suffragette and she could not get over being married and tied to the home. She had a positive thing about being tied down.' One of the few middle class wives to come from a large family recalled that her mother was continually irritable, 'but then what can you expect when she had all of us to look after? She lost my father very early.' The wife of an optician complained that her parents simply did not understand children. 'They were too fussy, forever nagging and really frightened of children in their hearts.' 46% of the wives were very critical although they were not prepared to say that they had been *extremely* unhappy. 'We were happy enough,' said the wife of a city clerk, 'but I must say our parents were very strict and punished us regularly. But then I don't suppose this was any worse than average.' The majority, however, recalled their childhoods with pleasure. 'We were always a happy family' and 'Yes, ours was a really happy childhood, I was always very attached to my parents and I still am,' were typical statements.

76% of those who *had* been critical of their childhood had subsequently established good relationships with their parents. Marriage often proved a turning point. 'I've only really got on well with my parents since I left home and married,' said one. The wife of a publican said that her relationship with her father had from childhood been one of continual conflict. 'But now I've a home of my own, he's at last prepared to leave me be.' The wife of an art teacher, whose parents were working class, found that going to university set up 'emotional problems between me and my parents. I grew apart from them, particularly my mother. But now I'm married it's a bit better, well we've things in common again.'

Education

As might be expected the majority of the sample were well educated, this being one of the factors that both differentiates working from middle class and promotes movement from working to middle class. 6% of the wives went to secondary modern schools which they had left by fifteen. The great majority, 65%, went to grammar schools, and 29% went to private schools. 67% stayed on till at least seventeen, and 27% left school at eighteen. Details of further education will be discussed under the section on 'Work', but it is worth noting at this point that 44% went on to some kind of full time further education and 35% entered into full time training for at least nine months after leaving school. In fact the two main differences between the backgrounds of the two samples centre around differences in size of the family of origin and differences in education.

Background to Middle Class Husbands

The average age of the middle class husbands was thirty-five, rather older than the working class men whose average was twenty-nine. The age range was twenty-four to forty and the median age thirty-two.

As had proved true of the entire sample the great majority were Londoners, 79%, a larger number indeed than their wives. (This may indicate, though the evidence here is slender, that while working class marriages tend to settle in the wife's locality, middle class marriages follow the husband.) 37% had parents who had also been born in London, and of those parents still alive, the great majority had moved out of London into the suburbs or farther afield. 33% of the men came from working class backgrounds.

45

Size of Family of Origin

Only one husband came from a family of six, and 23% were only children. 58% came from families of two children or less. In fact the families of the middle class husbands were the smallest in the entire sample, and the contrast between the size of the husband's family of origin, average size two, and his intended family size is even more marked than that of his wife, which may indicate a rise in the middle class birth rate.

Memories of Childhood

As with the working class sample this information comes at second-hand from the wife. But whereas three-quarters of the working class wives felt that their husbands' childhoods had been happy ones, rather fewer of the middle class wives, 60%, were able to say this. 40% were adamant that they have been unhappy. 'We are not on friendly terms with his parents even now. It's his mother he can't abide,' said a clerk's wife, 'and he left home early because she was reading all his letters.' 'Well, you see, he was an only child,' explained the wife of a civil servant, 'so he had pressure on him from all sides all the time.' For one husband social mobility had caused a break with his parents. 'They are a real working class couple,' said his wife, 'and he never had much in common with them. The whole family thought him a "bit funny". In the end they threw him out.' In fact 75% of the husbands with working class backgrounds were reported by their wives to have had unhappy childhoods. The reasons for this can only be guessed at. It may be that the cost of social mobility paid by a man is higher than that paid by a woman, who when her turn comes to bear and care for children has an automatic link with her mother. It may also be that a wife whose husband comes from a lower class feels hostility towards his parents, and this was reflected in the replies. However, in two cases, the wives also came from working class backgrounds and they had been reasonably happy in their own childhoods.

Education

As is true for the whole sample, the majority were state educated, but 40% of the middle class husbands went to private schools. Only 8% left school at fifteen (this includes all those who went to secondary modern schools) and 50% stayed at school until eighteen. 40% went on to university, and a further 23% to some kind of training college.

44% had gone into the professions which ranged from engineering to psycho-analysis; 12% of the whole sample were teachers; 17% were in business on their own account —which ranged from 'import-export' in the city to a small family picture-restoring business. 31% were managers or executives of all kinds, the majority in large companies. One man was a student of accountancy, one was an artist, and two were high level clerks. In fact this sample is probably a little biased in favour of the professions and business, and the 'lower' middle class of clerks and supervisors is under-represented. Incomes ranged from £17 per week to £5,000 per annum, but the average was around £1,500 per annum. Only one wife did not know what her husband earned and only one other felt she had no right to reveal her husband's income.

To summarise, the typical middle class wife of this survey was born in London as was her husband. Her parents were likely to be living in London, though her husband's parents were not. She is about twenty-seven years old, her husband a few years older, and both she and her husband came from small families. She is likely to be critical of her own childhood and of her husband's, but relations with *her* parents, at least, are reasonably good now. She stayed on at school until at least seventeen, and both she and her husband have some kind of further training or education. Her husband's income is in the range of £1,500 per annum.

Chapter Seven

HOUSING

THE quality of family life is greatly influenced by its standard of housing. As McGregor & Rowntree (1962) said, 'Income and housing are the main indices of the quality of family environment especially when there are young children.' P.E.P. (1961) in their survey of *Family Needs and the Social Services* found that housing was the service about which the largest number of complaints were received. 24% of their sample had serious housing problems, and 31% considered they had a problem.

In this survey the great disparity between middle class and working class housing is most striking, and shows that to solve one's housing needs on a low income without assistance in terms of subsidy, is very difficult in London.

The range of housing among the middle class families was very great—from a large detached house with six bedrooms, a nursery, study, dining room, separate sitting room, two bathrooms, etc., in three-quarters of an acre of grounds in one of the most fashionable areas of London to a small flat above a shop in a busy high street. But 71% lived in houses which they either owned already or were in the process of purchasing by mortgage. 87% of these houses were in small suburban roads, with an average of three bedrooms, one or two living rooms and a small garden. 21% of the families lived in flats, some of these very modern and elegant, but all the families living in flats intended at some point to move to a house. 'I like a flat, but when you've got children—well a house is more convenient,' was a typical comment, as was the remark that its 'always better to pay for something you're going to own yourself'. 8% of the families lived in 'working class style', that is in rooms without a separate entrance in a converted house. One family was lucky in having its own lavatory and bathroom, but the others faced the conditions so common among working class families, of sharing lavatories, and managing without bathrooms. All of them had every intention of moving, and two had already set in motion the process of buying a house, though in both cases it meant moving out of London into the country in order to do so. None of the middle class families were tenants of the Council. The position of the working class families in this survey was entirely different. 4% of the families lived in terraced houses which they owned and 2% of the families rented an entire house from the Council. 6% lived in private blocks of flats, and 17% in Council blocks. The majority, that is 71%, of the families lived in rooms. 87% of these were in small Victorian houses which had been divided up in recent years to house an average of three or four families. For those who were lucky enough to have had their landlords bought out by the Council—25%—things were not too bad as the Council was committed either to rehousing them or to modernising their existing accommodation. The conditions of those living in privately rented accommodation were noticeably lower than that of any other group. One of the worst off was the wife of a labourer who lived with her husband and twin sons of nine months in one room in which they cooked, ate, slept and spent their leisure. There was no bathroom and the lavatory was shared with all the other occupants of the house, numbering about ten. For this they paid £3 per week. 42% of the families lived in two rooms, one of which served as kitchen, living room and sometimes as a bedroom as well. For parents and children to sleep in the same room was commonplace. 71% of the families in rooms had no bathroom. 48% of them were sharing their lavatory with at least one other family, and in one case, the family lived over a small factory and had to share the lavatory during the day with the fifteen men employed in the factory. 53% of these families were without a bath and shared their lavatory. All but three of them were tenants of private landlords. Rents varied from 16/- to £5 and among those living in privately owned rooms there seemed no relationship between rent and facilities offered. Thus one family living in two rooms without a bathroom and sharing a lavatory were paying 19s. 6d. Two streets away another family was living in exactly the same conditions and paying £5. The great majority were extremely keen to move, though for most moving was more a dream than a possibility. Like their middle class counterparts, many working class mothers dreamt of a house. 'I'd move tomorrow if we could find something,' said the wife who lived over the factory, 'but we're tied because if we move my husband loses his job.' 'We're saving like mad to put seven hundred down on a house,' said the wife of a motor mechanic, 'but it's got to be a New Town; there's no hope for people like us in London.'

Just how difficult it is for a low income family with children to find accommodation in London was demonstrated by a survey made by the Family Services Unit for Kensington and Paddington. The trouble the Family Services Unit had in finding accommodation for a man, his wife and three children underlines how children complicated housing problems. P.E.P. in their study suggested that the criterion for need of this social service was 'the number of dependent children in the family'. Barbara Wootton (1959) called the low wage earner with young children 'a recent addition to the army of the "New Poor".' Zweig (1961) commented on the difference in standards of living between families with and without children: 50% of the childless families owned their own houses as compared with 6% of the families with four children. F. W. Miller etc. (1960), reported that 'families with young children were at a special disadvantage when compared with all families' and they found that the younger the children the worse the conditions. Donnison, etc. (1961), found that 77% of the group most badly housed were families with young children. Experience with homeless families underlines this fact: as John Greve (1962) says it is not large families that are the trouble—'the mere possession of children creates a serious disability, and if wages are also low then the chances of renting privately dwindle rapidly'.

Perhaps the worst case in this sample was a family of six. The husband was a plumber's mate. They lived in one room and a small kitchen in which the wife and her husband slept on a mattress on the floor. Repeated attempts by the doctor to get them rehoused on medical grounds failed, and as the wife said, 'There was only one thing left for me to do'—she had made an attempt at suicide. The relationship between bad housing and poor physical health is obvious. What is less well known is its effect on mental health. Yet a survey made in Cambridge in 1960 of the kinds of illnesses doctors cited in applications for the rehousing of the patients revealed mental illness as the most frequently given reason. Up till 1956 doctors could back appeals for rehousing with a medical certificate, and 126,000 such certificates were sent to the L.C.C. alone in 1956. After 1956 this was stopped, and doctors were permitted to apply to the County Medical Officer of Health only for cases of 'very severe medical condition aggravated by bad housing'. Despite this the number of urgent applications has steadily mounted.

In considering the impact of bad housing upon the quality of life, several points should be remembered. First, poverty is only relative; people's expectations and tolerance of their own conditions are affected by what they see around them. Thus many women commented on their 'bad luck' in not getting into a Council flat, and felt that their own inadequate accommodation was made to seem even worse through the knowledge that others no different from themselves, often relatives and friends, were able to live at a far higher standard for the same amount of money.

Secondly, the volume of traffic in big cities today makes

the kind of street life so common among slum dwellers of previous generations increasingly rare. Such street life is also dependent to some degree on a stable local population familiar with the area and each other, and a street level front door. But such conditions do not obtain in the majority of London boroughs today. Certainly in the areas around Kentish Town, there was nothing like it to be found, even in the one or two little pockets of stable populations. But for the majority of families in this survey, living in two or three rooms on the first or second floor of a tenement house in a street where they knew at worst no one, at best one or two others, there was no real escape. The point here is that the disappearance of street life confines the average young mother to her own home, a home she knows only too well is unsatisfactory, and which she no longer feels is the inevitable lot of her kind. Thus a situation which was difficult to start with is made doubly so by the factors just mentioned. The subject will be discussed further, when the lives of the children are analysed, but at this point what needs emphasising is that bad housing dominated the lives of over 60% of the working class sample. Any comparison of working class and middle class mothers cannot avoid highlighting the importance of this fact.

Chapter Eight

MARRIAGE

THE Registrar General in 1960 noted the reduction in the age at marriage, particularly since the Second World War, and that in 1960 more than one-quarter of all brides were under twenty. A recent study of teenage aspirations among school children by Veness (1962) revealed marriage to be mentioned by 94% of the girls. As Veness said the impression gained from the life histories was that 'being married was as inevitable as growing up', and is not seen in terms of status achieved, but as 'settling down' and 'rearing a family'.

For this sample the working class revealed a higher number of teenage brides than the middle class, 33% as compared to 12%. 98% of the working class girls had married before they were twenty-five. 75% of the middle class had married before the age of twenty-five. Class differentials in marriage patterns have always existed, and at present probably reflect the different life patterns of young people. Middle class adolescents who continue with their education are less likely to marry until they are at least twenty-one. It has also been suggested that the flight into marriage by the young working class girl is perhaps her only way of acquiring the outward signs of adulthood and a limited and temporary limelight. In Veness's life histories the details of the 'day' and dress were given frequently. Spinley (1953) has suggested that among the poorer working class areas there is simply no place for an unattached woman, and the combination of this lack of status, with the general overselling of the delights of 'falling in love' places enormous pressure on young girls to seek a mate.

It may also be partly explained by the ambiguity of our sexual morality. In public pre-marital sex is not condoned. In fact, with the age of puberty falling and knowledge of contraception spreading it is impossible to prevent. What is more the emancipation of women may have had an effect on the value placed on virginity. Anthropologists have noted that the more a society places women on a pedestal, as in modern Brazil or Victorian England, removed from the realities of life, the greater will the virginity of brides be prized. However, the less the division between male and female the less is virginity considered important, thus allowing young girls to experiment in the same way as young men. So the barriers to sexual liaisons among the young are growing weaker. But the pressure of public morality is still strong and the result may be that sexual relationships once entered into rapidly blossom into marriage even without the pressure of an unexpected pregnancy.

75% of the working class sample had a steady courtship for at least a year. This includes 75% of the teenage brides, which is an indication of how early 'steady' relationships were established. Only 6% of the working class married within three months of meeting their husbands. 87% of the middle class went steady for at least one year, and only 2% were married within three months. Friends provided the chief source for introductions for the working class, and college or school for the middle class. Clubs proved the second most important place for meeting amongst the middle class, dances came second for the working class. 29% of the working class married against their parents' wishes as did 19% of the middle class. The working class girls as a whole, however, were far less concerned about their parents' approval than were the middle class; 75% said that parental opposition would not have worried, and would certainly not have deterred them. Only 42% of the middle class wives felt able to be so independent. This is very interesting in view of the fact that the working class girl traditionally maintains a very close relationship with her mother who plays a role in her marriage that has not been so noted among middle class families. This might point to the greater alienation of the working class teenager from the adult world, which is not so greatly experienced by the middle classes who undergo a more prolonged period of dependence as a result of extended education. The 'teenage' world of the pop song and massmedia generally is still largely, though not entirely, working class. It is possible that this world swallows up the working class girl in the brief period between leaving school and marriage, cutting her off from her parents, and encouraging her to spend her relatively high earnings on cosmetics, clothes and records. Once married, however, the old relationship may be re-established.

In this sample, as has been said, 29% of the working class married against their parents' wishes yet 93% of these wives were now on good terms with their parents.

All the wives in the sample were asked whether they thought that they had married at the right age or not. 65% of the working class replied in the affirmative as did 79% of the middle class. Some middle class wives, however, did suggest, as the wife of a teacher put it: 'it was the right age for me but it would have depended on the person.' (She was twenty-one at marriage.) Another middle class wife, one of 12% who married as a teenager, said, 'I don't regret it but I wouldn't advise others to marry so young.' 'Yes,' said another, 'it was all right—you see I had been "around" so to speak since I was eighteen so I felt quite ready.' The wife of a carpenter who married at twenty-two said, 'I had my teenage years to myself—they're the best years of your life so I was fine.' Another working class wife said, 'Quite frankly I got fed up not being married, I was jolly pleased to do so, and to have children.' (She was married at seventeen.)

However, 35% of the working class wives felt they had married too young. 'I must have been mad,' said one. 'I didn't have a clue, my children will have to wait till they are twenty-one.' 'It's feeling so stuck what with the kids and everything,' said another who had married at twenty. 'Even if you've had your fling it doesn't make up for this tied down feeling.' 'It's the dancing I miss,' said one girl married to a skilled engineering worker. 'I'd like to have had more time for going dancing.'

Only 21% of the middle class sample felt they had married too young, but those who did were quite specific as to the reasons. 'I didn't have time to finish my training and make a career for myself. I would like to have either married much later or much earlier so I could have finished things before having my children.' (She married at twenty-three and had in fact been married twice—the first marriage lasting only a few months.) 'Yes, of course I was too young. But I had no choice, I wanted desperately to get away from my parents and this seemed the right way to do it.' For the wife of a salesman it was adventure she missed. 'I think by marrying at twenty I missed a great deal. I would like to have travelled.' Her husband, who happened to be present during the interview, was not much impressed with this point, remarking that in his opinion no one was ever 'old enough to get married'.

However, among both classes it did not appear that these complaints were directed specifically at the husbands. The general impression was that they had not really got the most out of their youth before settling down. This was particularly evident among the working class, for whom the gap between the single and married way of life seemed very great, as demonstrated by the girl who never went dancing any more. In fact, what was revealed was a lack of foresight and of real thinking as to what marriage entailed. Very few were 'forced' into marriage; only 10% of the working class wives gave birth to their first child within nine months of marriage, as did 6% of the middle class wives. In fact 46% of the working class and 48% of the middle class were married at least three years before their first child was born.

A psycho-analyst writing in a woman's magazine com-

mented on the lack of foresight that many young people
exhibit over marriage. She pointed out that she was constantly
being asked to treat unhappy married women, and suggested
that often 'after the excitement and expectations of adolescence, life is dull'. Slater and Woodside (1951) in their study
noted that in many cases the idea of marriage had been con-
sistently over valued, and expectations had been set too high.

However, in answer to a question asking whether they
considered their relationships with their husbands to be
more egalitarian than that of their parents, 56% of the working class and 65% of the middle class answered in the
affirmative. 'Emphatically there is more equality with us,'
said a teacher's wife. 'My husband doesn't help in the home
as much as my father,' said the wife of a copywriter, 'but
when it comes to sharing responsibilities—well then there's
no comparison, we are much closer.' Of course, this kind
of question meant different things to different people and
to the wife of a bank clerk equality meant giving each other
independence. 'We leave each other to go our own ways—
my parents could never have done that.' Amongst the
working classes, equality was often taken to mean closeness.
'We talk to each other you know—my parents never really
talked, what you might call closely, to each other.' 'My
father was Irish,' said the wife of a butcher's assistant, 'and
Irishmen don't do anything in the home—whereas my
husband—well he couldn't be better.' 'My father was never
home, not so as you'd notice, while my husband, well he's
home all the time and that makes for more sharing,' said
another wife.

On the basis of answers to the various questions on
marriage, which gave quite a detailed picture, three rough
categories were decided upon. Those who were reasonably
happy—that is showing no obvious signs of conflict—those
who were doubtful, and those who were clearly unhappy.
From this the middle class emerged as rather happier. 62%
of the middle class came into the first category. 'I began to
wonder whether I'd ever find the right person,' said a

business man's wife. 'I think I'm very lucky to have him,' was another comment. 'Some of my friends feel trapped but I don't, my husband is just right,' said the wife of a store manager. 'My husband encouraged me to come out of my shell, and he gave me all the support I needed.' Among the working class 54% seemed very happy. 'He'll do anything I ask.' 'He's always around when I need him,' were typical comments. Only two middle class wives seemed positively unhappy. The wife of a lecturer at a technical college was a little frustrated because her career had not worked out well and she felt that her husband had not given her the support she needed. The other wife felt that she and her husband had very little in common. 'We lead quite separate lives and never like each other's friends.' For the 17% of the working class wives who seemed unhappy, life was a series of constant rows. A railwayman's wife said, 'the trouble is he's a great Casanova, and can't understand being landed with me.' The wife of a builder's mate put it down to loneliness. 'I was so lonely in those early years, we lived in furnished rooms and never did anything but row. Though I'll say this, things are better now.'

Obviously this survey does not set out to give a detailed analysis of marriage in terms of personal compatibility—indeed this would be impossible without some detailed contact with the husbands. However, the surface information gained presents a fairly cheerful picture.

From the point of view of this research, the most interesting thing to emerge is that the conflicts which women experience as a result of the ambivalence of the feminine role do not appear in this sample at least to express themselves in terms of marital difficulties. As the next section will indicate it is children not marriage that present problems of role and expectation to the women of this survey.

Chapter Nine

MOTHERS AND CHILDREN

PART I: MIDDLE CLASS

31% of the families in the middle class sample had only one child at the time of the interview. 48% had two children, 21% had three. There were no families with more than three children. However, by no means all the families were complete. 4% of the sample wanted five or more children, and 21% intended to have four children. But 73% wanted to restrict their families to two or three children.

The same ambition was revealed by the school leavers studied by Veness. Three-quarters of the boys and girls wanted two or three children, three being the absolute favourite. Allowing for inaccuracy both in description and action, 85% were very firm in their contention that their families had been planned and would continue to be so. This accords with the most recent findings on the use of birth control in this country. Rowntree and Pierce (1961) found that 64·3% of their total sample fully approved of birth control, and the later the marriage the higher the numbers of approvers. This increase also applied as one ascended the class scale, 71% of non-manual informants approving as compared with 66·1% skilled manual and 58·1% unskilled.

There is also evidence from this sample that birth control was practised from the beginning. Only 19% of the wives had had children within the first eighteen months of their marriage, and 48% waited at least two years. This accords with the findings of Rowntree and Pierce who found that

58% of their non-manual sample most recently married began birth control at marriage. Rowntree (1962) later compared teenage brides married in the fifties with those married in the fifties but aged between twenty–twenty-four. 34% of the teenage brides began birth control at marriage, and 49% of the older brides did so. (N.B. The fact that a larger number of wives claim to have planned their families than appear to have done by a study of the interval between marriage and the first child, can be explained in part by the desire of some to have a child straight away.) In fact of the 15% of wives who said they had not planned their families only two had borne children in less than a year. Obviously birth control is a subject that is not always conducive to obtaining the complete truth, but it is fair to say that this sample reveals a great majority of wives consciously planning the size and timing of their families.

Previous Experience
The middle class women, as has been pointed out, came from small families, and thus opportunities for gaining experience with babies and small children were few. In fact 81% of the sample had had no experience with babies of any kind when they came to have their first child. Unfortunately, at the time the questionnaire was devised it did not appear to be necessary to ask the wives any further detailed questions on their experience or lack of it, and its impact on their lives. However, subsequent study has revealed that this may in fact be of great importance to the whole question of the changing position of women. A small study done by Belle Tutaev (unpublished) revealed the birth of the first child to be a major psychological turning point. The majority had had no previous experience, and found that health visitors, experts of all kinds, and most particularly husbands implied that they ought to know what to do. 'I felt such a failure as a mother,' said one young wife, 'not knowing whether the baby was warm enough, or fed enough, or why it was crying. I began to doubt that I could ever do anything properly

again.' Another said, 'I felt that I was a failure as a person too—and from this moment I began to feel lonely and displaced . . .' The Newsons (1963) comment that the problem is aggravated for the middle class mother who may have 'aspirations to an active intellectual life'. For such a woman the period when her children are very young 'may be a time of frustration and despondency'. However, the general impression gained during the interviewing indicated that the impact of the first child had a more detrimental effect on the *working class* than the middle class mother.

Help with the Children

One of the times that a family rallies together is on the arrival of a new member, and in fact 69% of the sample had help from a member of her family when she had her children, either in the form of housework, running the home, or caring for the older children. For 10% the only source of assistance was their own husbands. 46% had help from their mothers, and 12% had help from their mothers-in-law. Some people found the difficulty was to hold off the willing helpers. The wife of a sales manager who had her second daughter at home said, 'It was like a mad-house—my husband stayed home, my mother came, so did my sister, and so did my mother-in-law and my sister-in-law.' In fact as far as the organisational aspects of childbirth were concerned there were virtually no complaints.

Husband's Help

One of the most obvious reflections of division of roles within a family is the degree to which the husband participates as a father in the life of his children. An article in the *Daily Herald* as long ago as November 1953 commented that 'Young men are now family men in a way that former generations were not. They push prams, do the washing up and bath the baby.' The Newsons found a high degree of participation by fathers in the lives of their children, and this is certainly the case in this survey. 44% of the fathers would do, and in fact did everything required for their children from playing with them to soothing them when they cried at night, from feeding them to changing their nappies. A further 21% were rated very helpful by their wives, which meant they would do most things as a matter of course, but drew the line at one or two things, usually changing nappies. 'He just can't, he says he's too squeamish,' said a research scientist's wife. Then there was getting up at night. 'Well,' said a salesman's wife, 'he has to go to work so I can't really complain if he won't do that.' The majority of wives whose husbands came into these two categories were extremely appreciative of their husbands' behaviour. 'He's quite quite marvellous,' was a frequent comment. Very few took it for granted, and only one—a teacher's wife —expressed surprise that the question should be asked at all. 'It *would* be something to remark on if he *didn't* share the children with me,' was her comment. 31% of the wives rated their husbands as interested but not helpful. 'He's very good at entertaining them,' said the wife of a dentist, 'but when it comes to the technicalities, well he just doesn't want to know!'

'Well, we have a nanny,' said an executive's wife, 'so the question of him doing anything just doesn't arise. I don't expect he would, but he's certainly very interested in them and plays with them.'

Only 4% of the wives in the entire sample rated their husbands as non-participant. 'My husband is South American,' said one, 'and he considers it beneath his dignity to help or to be too interested in them as individuals. But he's jolly keen on having children as such.' In the other case the husband was a child-psychiatrist—curiously enough —and he 'hasn't got time. He works so hard he literally never sees them.'

How were they Bringing their Children up?
62% of the women in the sample felt that there was a clear difference between the way they had been brought up, and

the way they were bringing their own children up. In every case but one this emerged as a greater degree of consciousness of the needs of the child, and a greater degree of permissiveness. 'I give my children more freedom,' said the art teacher's wife. 'For example they call me by my own name.' 'I am not always fussing about good manners,' said the wife of a civil servant. 'I leave that kind of thing alone.' The bank clerk's wife was sure her way was better. 'My children get a great deal less minute supervision than I did,' she said 'and there is less will power exerted over them. I allow them to express themselves not repress themselves.' This increased freedom was referred to by others: 'My children have definitely more freedom to express themselves,' was one comment. 'My mother,' said another wife, 'brought us up to be good. We were very inhibited particularly sexually. I do, of course, try to give my children some moral values, but I don't want them to be inhibited.' This presents a different picture from that described by the Newsons, who found that while working class mothers tended to note differences, middle class mothers stuck to the same methods. Whether this represents differences between London and Nottingham, or differences between interviewer expectations is not really clear. However, it would seem to be a field worth studying, by students of both class and child rearing practices.

It is worth mentioning at this point, the view of Miller and Swanson (1958). They argue that over the past thirty or forty years middle class child rearing patterns in the United States have undergone three distinct changes. The first period—post Truby King—involved strictness, routine and self control, indeed socialisation according to the 'Protestant Ethic' in preparation for an individualistic social order, where success was dependent on one's ability to invest for tomorrow rather than spend for today. With the development of the large scale bureaucratic organisations, Miller and Swanson suggest, came a decline in the value attributed to self control. Welfare bureaucracy removed the need for competition and individualism. The powerful, the ambitious, the independent came to be frowned on, and the ideal bureaucratic or Organisation Man was 'warm, friendly and supportive of others'. This explains, say Miller and Swanson, the sudden change in middle class child rearing patterns from strictness to permissiveness, from stress on routine and self discipline to stress on relaxation and adjustment. Thus they argue there is positive encouragement of passive enjoyments such as thumb sucking—so frowned on ten years earlier—because they are aids to adjustment.

Recently, however, Miller and Swanson have suggested a new type of family pattern is emerging, as the 'Organisation Man' has fallen into disrepute. Within large scale organisations specialists have once again come to be considered of vital importance, and this is reflected in society at large where everyone is viewed in terms of his potential skills and abilities. This has brought about a renewed interest in limiting children's freedom, as democracy within the family is abandoned in favour of meritocracy. The value of adults as compared with children has been reassessed in favour of the adults, and 'baby experts' no longer urge parents to be 'buddies to their children'. The working class, Miller and Swanson suggest, are always one stage behind. When the middle class were so routine-conscious the working class were notably more permissive. Information trickled downwards, so to speak, and while the middle class were turning towards permissiveness, the working class were attempting to become more strict and regular. Now the middle class are turning towards a greater degree of strictness, the working class have just discovered the theories of permissiveness, and once again accord more freedom to their children than the middle classes do. This last point will be referred to in the section on working class children. The question to consider here is how relevant is this study of child rearing patterns to those in Britain, and to this study in particular. Unfortunately, we have no comparable study in this country, though the Newsons are attempting to fill the gap. Certainly this sample would indicate that the English are in the permissive phase.

37% of wives felt there was no change in their methods as compared to their mothers. In the majority of cases the reason for this was that their *own mothers had been self conscious permissive mothers*. 'My mother,' said the copywriter's wife, 'always read books on child care, and was very conscious of the way a child develops.' 'My parents,' said the actor's wife, 'always thought very carefully about us, and always let us have our way if they could.'

56% of the sample felt that their own children were having a better childhood than they had had. (This included 90% of those who felt their methods of upbringing differed from those of their parents.) 'I was evacuated,' said the wife of a sales manager. 'I missed my parents and was very unhappy—thank goodness there is none of that for my children.' 'I was brought up during the war,' said a laboratory technician's wife, 'that meant separation from my parents, no toys, no money, no comforts.'

'I was just plain lonely,' said a representative's wife. 'I was an only child and I *longed* for company. I shall certainly have a large family (she had two children already and planned to have another two). Jealousy too was mentioned. 'There was one real thing wrong with my childhood,' said one wife. 'I hated my half-sister—indeed I still do—it blighted my life. I am being very careful to prevent anything like that happening to my children.' Many mothers specifically referred to their methods of upbringing as paramount reasons why their children's lives were better than their own childhoods. 'I really try,' said a lecturer's wife. 'I actually try to do better and be more sensitive.' 'We've created a real family feeling,' said the wife of a television camera operator, 'instead as I was, part of a separate group called children, quite cut off from grown ups.' The participation of fathers was also a constant source of comment, being summed up by one wife who said, 'My children have a relationship with their father. I didn't!' 15% of the mothers did not feel that their children were having a better childhood than they had. One felt in fact it was worse. 'Although I may be a better mother,' she said, 'he lacks company, he doesn't see another child from morning till night—and when I do have the baby—well, it's not exactly going to be a playmate for him straight away.'

A teacher's wife also thought things were worse. 'From the point of view of being with me—well, perhaps things are better,' she said. 'I was evacuated. But we've always been so short of money, which my parents were not, so we can't get them any of the things I had. We feel very bad about this.'

The wife of an accounts executive was quite certain things were worse for her children because they were being brought up in London. 'Maybe I have a better attitude towards my children,' she said, 'but you just can't compare London to the life we had in the country—fresh air, freedom, animals, you just can't compare it.'

An engineer's wife also felt that life in the country was infinitely preferable, and expressed guilt about bringing her children up in London. Two others echoed the points about loneliness and lack of friends. 'He's an only child,' said a bank clerk's wife, 'and that makes him a little old fashioned and he lacks friends—there seems to be nowhere he can meet other children except at school.'

For the remaining 29% things appeared to be roughly the same. 'I muddle along just as my mother used to muddle along,' said the wife of an accountant. 'Who can say which is better or worse?'

Education

Everyone in the survey was asked what plans they had for the education of their children. As might be expected the middle class wives had rather stronger opinions and were more education conscious than their working class counterparts. As Jackson and Marsden (1962) point out this is because, in part, the schools of this country, state and private, embody middle class ideals, and this forms part of the middle class world. P.E.P. (1961) commenting on the fact that professional families have more than their fair share of grammar school education, said, 'They know more clearly what sort of education they want for their children, and they appear to get what they want. . . .'

Only 2% of the families did not consider education to be of prime importance, and for them it was education at school that they were not concerned with. Education at home they considered vital. 'Of course the children should go to school,' said the wife of a city clerk, 'but what is far more important is that we at home implant the right kind of moral values into the children. If they have those it doesn't matter what kind of education they have.'

One mother, while acknowledging the importance of educating her son well, said both she and her husband did not consider it of great interest as far as her daughters were concerned. 'We shall send the boy to boarding school,' she said. 'It doesn't really matter what we do with the girls.'

For the rest—96%—education was considered vital for both boys and girls, although there was considerable divergence of opinion about the relative merits of private and state schools, often within the same family.

'We consider education *the* thing,' said the sales manager's wife, 'and we are very against private schools. With the one reservation—of course—that we would not send them (two girls) to a secondary modern school if they failed the eleven plus.' 'Yes,' said one teacher's wife, 'schooling is vital. But the choice of schools depends on where you live. My husband is very against private schools; though I think they still have lots of advantages.' 'We consider private schools better at the moment,' said the civil servant's wife, 'but I don't think we'd consider boarding school.'

In fact 54% were determined to use the State system either from principle, or because of finance. 35% intended to use private schools, and 10% were waiting to see how their children developed. An interesting comparison can be made between intentions for the children and past schooling for themselves. In 40% of the cases both husband and wife were products of grammar schools. Of these 75% hoped to follow in their own footsteps and send their children to grammar schools. 15% both went to private schools and 100% of these couples intended to repeat their own experience and send their children to private schools. This may indicate that in our system of education, each type of school tends to claim its own kind as each new generation steps forward.

How Tied Down were They?
All but 6% of the wives had worked before they were married and only 10% did not continue to work after they were married. The birth of the first child, however, caused a much greater change than had marriage, and only 37% of the mothers had done any work since their first child had been born. With one exception they had all worked part-time. 44% of these mothers were working at the time of the interview. When asked if they considered they should be with their young children all the time, 40% replied in the affirmative. 'I used to think it wasn't important,' said a representative's wife, 'that is before I had children, but now, well up to three it's vital.' The artist's wife said much the same. 'I think, now I have a child, that it's very wrong for me to leave him. I used to think I'd go on working, but then I read articles and books about leaving little children and, well, I decided I would not.' 'My mother was always out,' said a general practitioner's wife, 'and I'm determined not to be like that with my children.' 52% of the mothers thought that provided they were home most of the time, and their arrangements were satisfactory, a small amount of separation from their mothers did their children no harm. In fact 17% of the families had full time living-in help, and another 10% had regular part-time help. 'I really can't see

the harm in it,' said a laboratory technician's wife, 'after all it's my mother who looks after them, and they really love her.' 'I wouldn't leave the children with just anyone,' said the store manager's wife, 'but someone they know well whom I trust, well, I think it's all right provided I'm home quite a lot.' Only 8% of the mothers in the sample considered their presence to be unimportant to the children. 'If they're too dependent on me,' said a businessman's wife, 'how can they go to school? No, I think it's a bad thing for children to be tied to their mothers.'

Certainly the general impression gained from the interviews was that despite the presence or absence of help with the children most mothers felt psychologically tied to their young children, and felt themselves compelled to stay at home whatever their own personal desires. 'Of course I must be with them all the time,' said a teacher's wife, 'though I must confess that sometimes I *long* to get away.'

27% of the husbands were most strongly opposed to their wives going out to work, and felt that their place was in the home with the children, and one or two others were recorded by their wives as having grave doubts on the subject, particularly when the children were below school age.

In fact full time schooling was clearly seen to be a turning point in the relationship between mother and child, and only 8% of the mothers were not fully determined to return to some kind of work once their youngest child was at school full time.

The subject of nursery schools was discussed. 33% of the families had at least one child at nursery school and only 12% felt they would not use one were a good one available. Many mothers complained that nursery schools were few and far between, and suggested that the State should provide more. It was clear that the motives behind these arguments were not a desire to 'dump' the children but rather to help them to get on with other children, provide them with friends, give them a change of atmosphere, and prepare the way gradually for school. 'I don't want to dump my child on anyone,' said one, 'but I would like him to meet some other children, and get out of this flat. He's no company to play with and the whole day is spent at home alone with me.'

If the day time is mainly dominated by the children, what of the evenings? As the Newsons point out, middle class wives in particular regard the evening as of great importance affording them the opportunity to function once more as independent adults. The evening is regarded as a time of adult activity and middle class wives long to go out, while, the Newsons argue, the working class wife is content to stay at home. In fact 67% of the wives in this sample went out at least once a week in the company of their husband, and only 17% were never able to go out with their husbands. However, of these 75% were able to go out on their own once a week. In fact there were only two mothers in the sample, 4%, who never went out at all.

To summarise, it can be said that the lives of these young mothers centred around their children and their home. There were indications that they were not fully prepared for the responsibilities motherhood imposed on them, and many were acutely aware of the restrictions it imposed on their lives. But their response to this was, in a majority of cases, to take the responsibilities of motherhood very seriously, and to devote to it much serious thought. Yet at the same time the majority were making a determined effort to keep up contact with the outside world, and thoughts about work often conflicted with desires to be good mothers. Only a small minority seemed really isolated in the same way as were the majority of working class mothers.

PART II: WORKING CLASS MOTHERS AND CHILDREN

It was pointed out earlier that despite differences in the size of their families of origin, both the working and middle class families were planning to have roughly the same number of children. A similarity can be seen also in the way the children are spaced. Both samples had been married on an average for $6\frac{1}{2}$ years, and family size can be seen to be very similar—although four working class families already have four children, and two have five or more. As can be seen, just under half the working class families have two children, sixteen have one child only, and eleven have three children or more.

		Present size	
No. of		MC	WC
Children		%	%
1		31	33
2		48	44
3		21	10
4		—	8
5+		—	4

Interestingly, however, far fewer working class mothers regarded their families as planned, in fact 71% said they were not. They indicated that birth control would be used to prevent any more children once the required number had been reached, rather than as a means of spacing and timing the birth of each child. Rowntree and Pierce (1961) noted that 'more couples of the poorer classes used contraception as a means of limiting rather than spacing births'. 33% of the wives had their first child within the first eighteen months of their marriage, as compared to 19% of middle class wives.

Previous Experience

As has been noted, many of the working class wives came from large families, and this was reflected by the fact that while only 19% of the middle class had had previous experience with children, 37% of the working class had had some experience. In two cases, this was because of previous work as a nanny, but for the rest, their experience was drawn from the family and contact with children of relatives. 'I was the youngest,' said a grocer's assistant's wife, 'and the story of my life has been helping out with my brothers' and sisters' children.' The wife of a sheet metal worker who had also been what she called the 'general help' for the family's children said, 'despite everything, when it's your own, well you feel different and you do worry more.' But the majority felt that their familiarity with children had helped enormously when it came to having their own.

The Newsons (1963) have noted class differences in the impact children make upon the life of a married couple. The working class wife, they argue, expects to find her main source of satisfaction in her family, and thus to become a mother is to achieve one of the things she wants, whereas the middle class wife expects to be an independent person in her own right, and thus finds that the presence of young children frustrates her from fulfilling what she considers to be her rightful role.

Certainly some of the evidence from this survey would tend to confirm this view in the sense that the middle class wives were consciously aware of the limitations imposed on them by their children, and thus were either accepting the situation deliberately, or making equally deliberate attempts to deal with it.

Among the working class wives there was an atmosphere of confusion and muddling through. Indeed it might have been just this atmosphere of muddle which led the Newsons apparently to contradict themselves, by stating that on the one hand the working class wife has expectations of life more suited to the rearing of children, than those of the middle class wife, and on the other hand saying that the middle class wives of their sample were more prepared for the appearance of a child than were the working class. They say, 'All the evidence suggests that middle class mothers . . . enter the experience of motherhood with more "enlightened" attitudes; and that they are likely to be more adequately prepared for the adjustments which the arrival of any new baby inevitably demands.' Yet some forty-eight pages later they say '. . . so many middle class mothers seem to see the period of infancy in particular not as a time of fulfilment, but as an abnormal, and in many ways deplorable interlude in an otherwise sane and well ordered life.' This may reflect both the authors' ambivalent ideas about the impact of motherhood, and those of the mothers in their survey. The same ambivalence was revealed in this study, reflected by a combination of thought, preparation and self-consciousness towards motherhood on the part of middle class mothers combined with a feeling that it is their right to be something more than 'just a mother'. Among working class mothers, motherhood was, as the Newsons suggest, expected and accepted as normal, and yet in some ways their ability to keep their heads above water as mothers appeared considerably less than that of their middle class counterparts. The factors contributing to this situation include bad housing, lack of play facilities, lack of nursery schools, lack of baby sitters, reduced contact with their extended family, and reduced earning capacities.

Help with the Children
As with the middle class, the great majority of the working class wives, 83% received help from their families at the time of their children's births. The wife's mother was the source of assistance in 35% of cases, the husband in 19% and the mother-in-law in 17%.

The Newsons found that the organisational aspects of childbirth more often went wrong among working class than middle class families, and that more working class mothers have their children at home than middle class, with all the disadvantages that a small and ill-equipped home can create. Only 4% in this sample felt that their experiences had been so bad as to put them off having any more children. For the majority, the difficulties and confusion seemed a fairly normal part of their lives. However it is worth noting that while none of the middle class mothers lost a child at birth, four of the working class mothers had their babies die in childbirth, which is in line with the class differential in infant mortality rates noted most recently by the National Birthday Trust.

Husband's Help

As with the middle class families, the degree to which the father participated in the lives of his children was quite striking, and the degree of participation was even greater than among the middle class families. 52% of fathers were rated by their wives as doing anything and everything for their children as a matter of course. A further 27% were prepared to do most things, drawing the line as did some middle class fathers over changing the nappies, and getting up at night. (The impression was gained that, among working class fathers in particular, the sex of the child played an important part in whether the father would change nappies or not. Many apparently doting fathers were very reluctant to perform this service for their daughters while being quite happy to do it for their sons.) Of the remainder, 21%, 12% were considered 'interested but not helpful' and just over half to be uninvolved in their children's lives. 'He's never really been what you might call interested,' said the wife of a grocer's assistant, 'although he wanted kids right enough.'

The controversy over who helps more, the middle or working class father, has not yet been entirely settled. For this sample it is clearly the working class father, yet in the *American Journal of Sociology* M. J. Kohn (1963), reports that middle class husbands are more participant. He argued 'few working class fathers do much to relieve their wives of the burden of caring for their children all the time'. Some of the confusion appears to have arisen by not taking into account different patterns of behaviour within the working class. The Newsons found for example that 57% of Class I and II fathers were highly participant, 61% of III white collar, 51% of III skilled manual, 55% of IV and 36% of V.

In this sample the most participant group was the skilled manual group. Obviously the whole subject of the contribution of husbands to their children's care needs to be further explored. The working class mothers appeared a little surprised, and very grateful for the assistance they were getting. 'He's simply wonderful,' said a carpenter's wife, 'in fact I'd say he's better than me. I often wonder how I'd manage without his help. The answer is that I couldn't!'

If there were more helpful husbands among the working class sample, there were also a slightly higher number of unhelpful ones. They tended as with those studied by the Newsons to be in Class IV or V and the majority felt that 'it was not their job to fuss around with the children' (the wife of a window cleaner).

How were They Bringing their Children up?

69% of the working class mothers felt they were bringing up their children differently from the way in which they had been brought up, and in 88% of cases this meant again less restriction and more understanding. 'My parents were always on at me.' 'In fact my father used to really knock me about. I certainly hope not to be like that,' said the wife of a sheet metal worker. 'My Dad was a really hard man,' said a labourer's wife, 'there was no affection in him. We are not like that at all.' 'My Mum was out all the time,' said a bus driver's wife. 'I know she had to but she never seemed to be thinking of me. I really concentrate on my children.'

This heightened consciousness of parenthood amongst working class as well as middle class rather points against any evidence of a cultural lag. However, as many of the interviews took place with the children present, some impression was gained incidentally of patterns of rearing. (It is interesting to note that the middle class mothers made every effort to have their children occupied elsewhere during the interviews.) It appeared very obvious that in a great many cases there was a difference between what the mother said she did, and what she actually did. On three occasions during three interviews a child was smacked by a mother who stated firmly that she never smacked her children. Spinley (1953) has suggested that the working class parents attempts' to control the child are very inconsistent. This theory of inconsistency was also suggested by Bronfenbrenner (1958) who pointed out that some of the apparent differences in patterns of child rearing which contrast the rational middle class parent with the uninhibited impulsiveness of the working class parent, may be due to differences not in aim, but in effectiveness. His own research, he said, indicated that the working class attempted to follow the same ideals as the middle class but that their method was considerably less effective. Certainly impressions gained from the children-parent relationship amongst the working class in this sample confirm this view. In conversation the working class mothers sounded very like the middle class in their attitudes to their children. In practice, however, they appeared more aggressive, and less in control, than their words suggested.

The remaining 31% felt there was no real difference between their methods and those of their parents. However, it is interesting to note that, despite the supposed strong tie between working class mothers and daughters, slightly more working class mothers than middle class drew attention to differences between themselves and their parents. 96% of the mothers were quite certain that their children were having a better childhood than they had had, material and psychological reasons being equally numerous. A London transport worker's wife was positively indignant about the difference. 'Blimey,' she said, 'I should say they are better off. We didn't have the liberty they have in their home, and what about the pictures, television, pocket money—they really have the lot!' 'I'm going to have less children,' said a taxi driver's wife. 'It's as simple as that, so my children will have more of my time and more of my money.' 'I'm not a nagger,' said a dustman's wife, 'but my Mum was, and she never stopped from morning till night-time.' 'Materially,' said the wife of a foreman, 'there is no comparison, look at our flat. (They had a particularly well equipped Council flat in a small block surrounded by large gardens.) We never had anything like this as a child.'

Only 4% of the mothers felt things had been better for themselves. In both cases it was the virtues of the country which were extolled. 'You just can't compare living in London to living in the country,' said one, 'it was so much healthier and cleaner in the country, and more fun.' For the other it was not only London versus the country but London versus the Italian lakes. 'I think most of all my children lack space, space to do what they like,' she said.

Education

The subject of the working class and education is now one that has been greatly discussed, and has resolved itself into a discussion of the ways in which education can be opened up to the working class. Many sociologists have argued that the 'ethos' or spirit of our educational system is an expression of middle class ideals, and its organisation is geared to middle class occupational needs. This provides a psychological barrier to working class entry, and forces those working class children who have broken through the barrier to 'choose' as Jackson and Marsden (1962) point out between home and school. This argument can in fact be slightly overstated, in that all children who seek more education than their parents have received will be faced with psychological difficulties. Also the middle class ideology to which the education system is attached is by no means desired or enjoyed by many sections of the middle class. However, this survey does confirm the rather different attitude to education among working class parents as compared to middle class, whatever may be the reasons.

37% of the mothers in this sample said that both they and their husbands did not consider education to be important. 'I'm doubtful about schools,' said a factory worker's wife, 'and I will never force them to stay on at all if they don't want to.' (She had a girl and a boy.) 'I never liked school,' said a plumber's wife, 'and I don't see any reason why they should either' (she had four children, two boys and two girls). A further 19% thought education important for boys but less so for girls. (Interestingly only one middle class wife made this distinction, although they were all given the opportunity to.) 'Yes,' said a greengrocer's wife, 'we shall see that the boy works hard at school, but with the girl, well it doesn't really matter anyway.' 'My husband is even considering sending the boy to a private school if he doesn't do well at the local one,' said a foreman's wife. 'I'm glad we've got only one boy, not two, because we shan't be so worried about the girl.' The remainder, just under half, considered education important, and hoped their children would do well at school. 'Well, you can't manage today without an education,' said the wife of a dress cutter. 'I feel it myself, not having really bothered.' 'My husband's particularly keen they should do well,' said a bus conductor's wife. 'He only went to the old elementary school, and feels he did not really have a chance.'

Thus, while 96% of the middle class sample was education-conscious only 44% of the working class sample really valued education. Indeed the fact that just under half the sample were very education-minded is quite surprising, particularly in view of the husband's and wife's own educational background, 73% of the wives and 75% of the husbands having left school at fifteen. H. Himmelweit has noted that while the working class were under represented in the grammar schools, 63% of the lower working class interviewed dreamt of at least lower middle class jobs, and 73% of the upper working class did so. Veness (1962) found that the majority of her school children hoped their children would do better than themselves. Yet as the Crowther Report pointed out, 42% of National Service recruits in the top 10% of ability left school at sixteen. This is not the place to go into the whole problem of how to help working class children make use of education. The difficulties in fact may go far beyond conflicting ideologies, into the ability to use language itself, and a culturally deprived child is at a disadvantage in any education system.

In the working class sample it appeared that the value placed on education was based less on past experience than had been the case amongst the middle class, and more on present attitudes to life and society and the general environment in which the couple was living.

How Tied Down were They?

Only one of the working class wives had not worked before marriage, and only 10% did not continue to work after they were married (in the majority of cases the reason for stopping was pregnancy). However, the birth of children proved a great deterrent, as it had to the middle class, and only 29% had attempted to work again since the birth of their first child. Whereas the majority of the middle class who continued working had organised regular part-time work for themselves, with the working class it was rather a temporary attempt to return to full time work which in every case failed, or was discarded. Only 36% of those wives who continued working had organised regular (i.e. more than three months) part-time work for themselves. For example one wife took her child twice a week to 'clean' at another house. Another worked four evenings a week as an usherette in a local cinema.

Many more of the working class felt they should be with their children all the time when they were young than did the middle class; 79% in fact as compared with 40% of the middle class. 'They fret if you leave them,' said a printer's wife. 'I did try when the boy was six months old, but he fretted, and was really unhappy, so I saw it was really wrong to try.' 'When they are young,' said a removal worker's wife, 'children need their mother, and it's doing them a wrong if she isn't there.' Only 10% thought their presence unimportant, and the others, 8% thought it all right provided, as a post office worker's wife said, 'I'm around when I'm needed.' 40% of the husbands were anxious that their wives should stay at home.

Whether this class difference in attitude towards leaving the children is based on genuine feelings or simply the knowledge that there are no adequate alternatives is hard to say. None of the working class families had the advantage of living-in help, nursery schools are mainly privately run, and expensive, and the few State nursery schools in London have long waiting lists. None of the working class children of the right age were at nursery school, although 79% of the mothers said they would like to make use of a State nursery school or play centre, were one available. However, it was clear that this was not to get rid of the children, but in the main to provide them with opportunities to play.

'It's so cramped in these two rooms,' said the post office worker's wife, 'they are on top of each other, and me all the time. As it is I have to take them out every afternoon whatever the weather.'

'It's the noise they make,' said a milk roundsman's wife, 'I have to keep telling them to be quiet, and they need somewhere where they can let off steam.' 'I'd like them to go to nursery school as a kind of training for school,' said the bus conductor's wife, 'you see they never play with any other children.'

This discussion revealed the very real problem facing the working class mother who may have three children under five at home all day. One wife in particular with two difficult and noisy children, living in two small rooms at the top of a house, felt this to be the major problem of her life. Hilda Jennings (1962) noted this problem. In the past, she said, the children had played in the street—'near enough at hand for an eye to be kept on them from the open door, from which mothers and neighbours emerged when there was a quarrel or an accident.' Then they moved into flats, and there was nowhere to play except indoors, and for the vigorous under fives who demanded active play, the act of controlling them caused stress and strain. Several mothers,

Jennings noted, were suffering from nervous strain which they said was a 'result of trying to keep their children quiet and safe'. This nervous strain was evident in several cases in this sample. Recently the problem of where children play has received some attention. Joan Maizels (1961) did a study of *Two to Fives in High Flats,* and found many mothers very worried by the problem. 'They feel hemmed in when they have to stay in all day.' 'He doesn't mix . . .' 'Makes him nervous'. 'They're too restrained at home, then they go mad when we're out,' were typical comments.

In fact the majority of this sample were tied to the children during the day in a way that the middle class mothers were not. If there was no neighbour or relative available then it was impossible to leave them, even for a hair wash and set, and 77% of the mothers mentioned that their children's need to play was a problem and worry for them.

31% of the working class couples never went out at all in the evenings. 12% of the mothers could not go out with their husbands as there was no baby-sitting arrangement available, so they let their husbands go out without them. This meant that 44% of the mothers never went out in the evenings. Of the 56% who were able to go out only 54% went out regularly once a week with their husbands, as compared with 67% of the middle class mothers.

In conclusion, it can be said that although the middle class mother may encounter psychological difficulties concerning her role as an individual with her first baby, she very soon makes a deliberate effort to assert her own rights as an individual. The working class mother who sees motherhood as inevitable is in fact less prepared for the ties of children and is less able to cope with the isolation that follows.

Chapter Ten

THE RUNNING OF THE HOME

PART I: MIDDLE CLASS

THE annual report of the National Food Survey of 1952 reported that the majority of wives understated their husbands' incomes by about 15%. In only one instance in this survey did a wife not know what her husband earned. 'I just don't know,' said a businessman's wife, 'the house was given us by his parents, he works with his father, so I've never really found out.' In every other case, all financial questions were quite open, although several wives admitted that they would be hard put to name an exact figure for their husband's income as 'perks' were involved, such as expenses, or a car on the company. Incomes varied from £5,000—the highest—to £17 per week—the lowest. 42% of the sample were living on incomes of less than £1,500 p.a. 29% earned between £1,500 and £2,000 p.a; 15% between £2,100 and £3,000 p.a;. 10% between £3,100 and £4,000, and 4% over £4,000.

54% of the wives drew a regular housekeeping allowance from their husbands' income which they tried to adhere to, although as a teacher's wife said, 'there are weeks when it just seems to go, and then I have to borrow money from Jim.' One wife said that she was really in charge of finances, and her husband simply took pocket money for himself from the bank, keeping the amount as small as possible. For the remaining 44% it was simply a case of drawing money when they needed it.

As far as the making of important financial decisions was

concerned, there was complete unanimity among the wives that this was always a joint affair arrived at after joint discussion, and this was true even of the few wives who were anxious to indicate that their husbands 'still wore the pants'.

Division of Labour within the Home

21% of the couples simply shared the housework, and the husband did any household chore required, from ironing to washing nappies, from cleaning to cooking. In every case the wife remarked on how much more helpful her husband was than her father had been (indicating a change in patterns of family behaviour). All of these helpful husbands were also rated as helpful with their children, which reveals a great deal of role sharing among these families. It was also clear that the majority of these wives, though grateful for the help given, also regarded it as their due. 'I would certainly consider myself hard done by if he didn't share the running of the house with me,' said the actor's wife. A further 44% of the husbands had certain tasks which they always did as a matter of routine, such as bedmaking at weekends or washing up the evening meal. All these husbands were willing to do more if required, and were considered very helpful by their wives. In every case but one, this was thought to be an improvement on the behaviour of their fathers. 'My father was an exception,' said the wife of an articled clerk, 'he was at home a great deal so he just had to help.' These husbands were prepared to do more if asked. 'He used to help more,' said the store manager's wife, 'but now he's working so hard, I tend to leave him alone.' 'He's often very tired,' said the publican's wife, 'so I don't really ask unless I'm desperate.' 'He would help more at weekends,' said the wife of a businessman, 'but now we employ domestic help, well I don't see the need for it.'

19% of husbands would wash up but nothing else. 'He's so unwilling to do anything,' a solicitor's wife said, 'that I

just make a point about washing up, and leave it at that.'
'He looks pretty sour if I suggest anything other than drying
dishes so I don't,' said the bank clerk's wife. 'Maybe he
would do more,' said a teacher's wife, 'but somehow I
doubt it.' One wife was quite content. 'He dries the dishes,
and helps with the children and that's all—but it's quite a
lot!' The remainder, 17% of the husbands, would never
help. 'My husband simply doesn't believe in doing housework,' said the optician's wife, 'but I do have help so I can't
really complain.' 'He just won't ever do housework,' said
the wife of a copywriter, 'but he makes up for it being a
very good handyman, and mending things.' It was interesting to note that these wives tended to be slightly apologetic
about their husbands' lack of helpfulness, not one of them
felt it to be the man's right to be waited upon in his own
home. The majority of these fathers were also not very
participant with their children. There seemed to be no particular relationship between not helping and social background, not even with income, although those with full
time domestic help clearly had less need of their husband's
assistance. The general overall impression is of a great deal
of sharing of household tasks, which in 56% of cases was
felt to be an improvement on the behaviour of the wife's
father.

A factor which further emphasised the home consciousness of the husbands was the number who had been
involved in the decoration of their home. 35% of
couples had decorated their home together, and in a
further 25% of cases this had been done by the husband
alone.

It is possible to conclude that the wives whose husbands
helped them took this as a matter of course, while those
whose husbands did not felt called upon to give a reason
for it. It is interesting to note that the wives did not take
their husbands' help with the children nearly so much for
granted, and constantly expressed their gratitude for their
husbands' assistance.

PART II: WORKING CLASS

6% of the wives said they didn't know what their husbands earned, and the wife of a grocer's assistant was quite certain she did not want to know. 'Well it's not my business, is it?' she said. The rest, however, regarded it as their business, and with one exception, were quite happy to reveal the exact amount. The highest income was a minimum of £30 per week and 'often it's near £45', said one wife whose husband ran a small newsagent's shop. Of the rest 10% earned over £20 per week, 31% earned between £15 10s. and £20 per week. 12% earned £10 or less, and the remainder, 33%, earned between £10 10s. and £15 per week. One wife whose husband was in prison was living on National Assistance.

Working class wives were more inclined to regulate their housekeeping money, and 77% of the wives took a regular amount from their husband's pay packet each week, and tried to make do with it. The rest, 23%, just shared it out as needed. 'In fact I do very well out of it, because my husband takes virtually nothing,' said a postman's wife, 'but then of course I've had it if I run out!'

In 10% of families the husband was the one who made all the important financial decisions. 'I never understand money so I wouldn't be much help,' said the newsagent's wife. 'Money is not a woman's business,' said another. For the others, 90%, as with the middle class families, financial decisions were always made jointly. 'We discuss everything,' said the wife of a skilled engineer, 'and we don't ever do anything we don't agree on.' 'We always talk it over first,' said a carpenter's wife, 'unless of course he's buying me something as a surprise!'

Division of Labour within the Home

54% of the working class couples (as compared to 21% of middle class) simply shared the housework between them, with no division into man's work or woman's work. 25%

of the husbands did regular tasks and would do more if asked, though many wives tended not to. 'We live in two rooms and I don't work,' said a window cleaner's wife, 'well, it wouldn't be right to ask him to start cleaning when he's been working all day.' This was a common point made by those who 'didn't ask', that is that they could manage without their husband's help. 'If we had a house,' said the wife of a sheet metal worker, 'well then it would be a different matter.' 12% of the husbands did the washing up as a matter of course. 8% did nothing, although it was not a matter of principle, but rather of just avoiding things. 'He'd wash up and grumble,' said a foreman's wife. 'He might even make a bed if I nagged, but he's not exactly what you'd call domesticated.' 'It's a question of time,' said a labourer's wife, 'he's never around at the times when I might really need help.'

As with the middle class sample the majority of helpful husbands were helpful with the children too. In fact 31% of the working class sample shared the running of the home, and the children completely. The majority of the working class wives, 67%, noted that their husbands were more helpful than their own fathers had been. 'My father never did a thing,' said one, 'even though my Mum had five children on her hands.' Again this is evidence of the shift in family patterns over the previous generation.

As might be expected, more working class husbands than middle class decorated their homes. In fact only 8% of the husbands out of the total had *not* done their own decoration. 62% did it on their own, but 29% had the assistance of their wives. This home decoration tends to confirm the popularity of 'Do it yourself' among the working class. Willmott (1963) noted this at Dagenham. 'Everybody seems to be a handyman on this estate,' said one of his informants, and although the L.C.C. were committed to redecorating every five years the majority spent a lot of time improving their homes. Usually decorating the home involved painting and papering the walls with contemporary wall paper, building cupboards and book shelves, and putting down linoleum on the floor. Often the result was a transformation of small dark rooms into cheerful, bright looking rooms whose basic discomforts had been well disguised.

In conclusion it can be said, that while both samples appeared to be very family minded and home centred, this was particularly true of the working class where the majority of fathers seemed as involved in the care of their home and family as did their wives.

Chapter Eleven

SOCIAL CONTACTS

PART I: WORKING CLASS

A great deal has now been written about the role of the extended family in working class life, and in particular about the relationships between married women and their mothers. Previous studies have revealed that in long settled working class areas relationships with extended families form a vital part of everyday life with especial emphasis on contacts between mothers and married daughters. As McGregor and Rowntree (1962) say, ' "Mum" emerges as the dominant figure within the extended family circle,' probably because 'the mother evokes a warmer and more loyal response from her young children than the father, teaches her daughter essential domestic skills, and is valued after the daughter's marriage as an adviser on household matters and as a grandchild minder'.

In the sample there is evidence of an extremely close relationship between husband and wife (unlike Ship Street as described by Kerr (1958) where the maternal grandmother dominated her daughters' marriages). There is not the clear division into man's world and woman's world that is part of traditional working class life. Nor is the area in which the families live a particularly stable one in terms of residence as was Ship Street or St. Ebbes or Bethnal Green.

In fact 43% of the wives had both parents living in the area (within a radius of one mile of their home). A further 8% had their mother only living in the area—the father being dead. Thus over half the wives had mothers within

88

easy access. Of these 28% saw their mothers every day. (That is 15% of the total.) But a soldier's wife who was actually living in her mother's flat as her husband was posted in Germany would like it to have been less. 'We seem to get on each other's nerves,' she said. 52% saw their mothers more than once a week (27% of the total), but again two couples were not too happy about this. 'We go there every Saturday,' said the wife of a plumber's mate, 'though I'd rather not, there's always an argument going on at my Mum's. It's better when she comes here.' A van driver's wife also could have happily seen less of her mother. 'She comes here on a Tuesday, but we are a bit touchy together sometimes, and I can't say I'm always sad when she goes.' The remaining 20% of wives with mothers living nearby saw their mothers irregularly, averaging once every two months. In 8% of cases both parents were dead. This left 48% of wives whose parents were not within very easy reach. Of these 17% saw their mothers more than once a week (8% of the total sample), 9% saw their mothers regularly once a week (4% of the total sample) and the remaining 74% saw their mothers less often (35% of the total). Some of the wives who had little contact with their mothers would like to have had more. An electrician's wife for example said, 'I'm lonely and I could do with some company.' But as many as 41% of these wives were reasonably content about the situation. The most usual complaint of those who were separated from their parents and their husband's parents as well was that there was no one to leave the children with. Certainly the general impression was of a focus of interest on the nuclear as opposed to extended family.

62% of the wives also had at least one sister living in the area, and several had two or three, and 13% of these met their sisters every day (8% of the total). 'We are as thick as thieves,' said a bricklayer's wife of herself and her two sisters, 'it's us against the rest you might say.' A further 47% met their sisters regularly more than once a week

(29% of the total). Indeed it appeared to some extent that relationships with sisters were more valued than with their mothers, and certainly there seemed to be a great deal of mutual baby minding among sisters. Contact with brothers appeared to depend on how well the wives' brothers got on with their husbands and though 31% of the wives had brothers living nearby contacts did not appear to be regular, except for the wife of a bus conductor, 'I met my husband through my brother and they are still the best of pals, so we see him often.'

58% of the couples were living near the husband's parents. Indeed there was no strong evidence from this sample to support the findings of Kerr and Young and Willmott who found young couples gravitating towards the wife's mother. 11% of these wives saw their mother-in-law every day, and they all would have liked such contact to be less frequent. One wife lived in the same house as her husband's parents who occupied the ground floor while they lived on the first floor. 'They never did a thing for us even when my husband had an accident, and we are not really good friends.' A postman's wife also shared a house with her husband's parents and said, 'They are very good to us, but even so we never seem to have our own life.' 28% of the wives with their husbands' parents nearby saw their parents-in-law more than once a week, and 53% met regularly at the weekend.

In 10% of cases the husbands' parents were both dead, leaving 31% whose parents were alive but not living close by. In every case contact was once a month or less.

40% of the husbands had sisters living in the area, and in 32% of cases the wives and the sisters-in-law met more than once a week. 'Either we meet at the shops,' said a milkman's wife, 'or she comes here, we got on real well.' Contact with sisters living further afield was less regular, and it was a case of meeting if a reason arose. 'We see Joe's sisters at Christmas,' said the wife of a navvy, 'but we don't seem to meet much during the year.'

35% of husbands also had brothers living nearby and 48% of the husbands saw their brothers at least once a week, though often this was at work, but contact between wives and husbands' brothers was very irregular. In fact meeting relatives appeared mainly to take place during the day, and appeared to be a case of men meeting men and women meeting women. Despite the fact that the majority of couples appeared to ignore the division between male and female roles within their own nuclear family, social contacts were still made separately rather than as a unit.

The question of friends is a difficult one when considering working class patterns of life, as friendships do not appear to be conducted in the same way as in middle class life. Some wives felt that they knew a lot of people but would not regard any of them as friends, the idea of a friend being something so special that few could live up to it; as a carpenter's wife said, 'to my mind the only friends you really have is your own Mum and Dad, and your husband if you are lucky, which I am.'

Certainly the majority of studies of 'old style' working class life reveal working class friendships to be family and neighbourhood bound, less a conscious choice than a passive acceptance of those who are available—i.e. neighbours. Indeed a great deal of the distress amongst working class couples who are rehoused in New Towns may be due to the fact that they have never learned the social skills involved in making new acquaintanceships and transforming these acquaintanceships into friendships.

However, the majority of wives in this sample were young enough to still have some friends from before their marriage, and so it was decided to question them about friendship in order to be able to make a comparison with middle class patterns. 25% of the wives said that neither they nor their husband had any friends at all. 'I don't really believe in mixing,' said the wife of a butcher's assistant, 'and nor does my husband, perhaps we would if we found our own type, but we don't seem to.' 40% said they had one or two'—these were usually their own friends rather than friends of themselves and their husbands', and they would visit them or go shopping with them during the day. A gardener's wife, for example, had one school friend, married, who lived nearby and they would go shopping together, or go out on the Heath together in the summer. Not one of the wives who said they had 'one or two' friends ever had their friends visit them in the evening. There was a substantial minority—35%—who replied that they had 'lots of friends'. 'We seem to be a sort of centre,' said the wife of a carpenter, 'people turn up here at all hours of the day and night.' Most of these 'sociable' couples had friends visit them in the evenings, and the majority felt that their friends were also their husbands'. 'Either we both like a couple,' said the wife of a post office sorter, 'or we both don't.' 25% of these couples always went on holiday with friends, and the same percentage go out with friends when they went out in the evenings. 'We were a gang, our lot,' said a motor mechanic's wife, 'and somehow we've all stuck together.'

Neighbourliness

The traditional working class attitude to neighbours as discovered by studies of long settled areas is one of great warmth illustrated as Hilda Jennings noted by a description of a street as being 'we are one big family.' Certainly it appears that an area needs to be settled for several generations before this atmosphere of warmth can develop. Indeed the majority of studies of New Towns have noticed the reduced neighbour contact as compared to the areas from which the 'settlers' have come. Young and Willmott found a great deal of fear and resentment towards neighbours in Greenleigh: 'It's like a strange land in your own country,' said one informant. The reasons for this loss of neighbourliness in new surroundings are many. It is in part, as has been suggested, an inability to utilise the necessary social skills for making friends, skills which were unnecessary in the old area. The most comprehensive discussion of this problem is probably that by Jennings (1962). She argues that any study of a long settled area will reveal a history of tensions, difficulties and unfriendliness, and that a 'community spirit' emerges out of this only very slowly.

However, it may be that the younger generation (and this study points in this direction) have genuinely shifted their pattern of living from a neighbourhood centred life to a family centred life. Mogey suggests this to be the case, and points out how this is reflected in increased participation of the husband in the daily routines of the household (as this study has shown), and with an increasing emphasis on the individual family a desire to form new friendships in middle class style (again this study confirms this).

Without a doubt neighbours played a relatively unimportant part in the lives of these couples. Only 29% of the wives said they had any contact with their neighbours at all. 'They are a good lot,' said a tube driver's wife, 'and we often meet for a cup of tea.' However the great majority, 71%, said they had no contact at all. 'They are all old people,' said a printer's wife, and the wife of a labourer also complained 'there are no young people around.' An electrician's wife felt her street was positively hostile. 'They'd cut your throat sooner than talk to you in the street round here,' she said.

To summarise, the picture that emerges of the social life of the working class couples in this sample is rather different from that depicted by the Institute of Community Studies. For example Young and Willmott found that in Bethnal Green the household of a young wife often 'merged' with that of her mother. They concluded that family relationships, and in particular the mother-daughter relationship, were a vital means of connecting people with their community. Evidence of the importance of the extended family was revealed in the very different area of Woodford, and in Dagenham where Willmott (1963) found that it played almost as great a part in people's lives as it had done in the East End.

However, in this study a picture emerges of a rather isolated, extremely family centred existence, with the focus not on the extended family but on the nuclear family. 33% of this sample, as has been seen, never went out in the evenings, extended family relationships were fairly widespread but not enveloping, and friends were the exception not the rule. It appears that the period when children are young is for many working class couples one of isolation, and withdrawal into the home during which time the main contact with the outside world is via television. In fact Young and Willmott noticed the great increase in television sets in Greenleigh as compared to Bethnal Green where 32% had TV sets. In Greenleigh it was 65%. 'The tellie keeps the family together. None of us ever have to go out now,' said one father proudly.

PART II: MIDDLE CLASS

Far less has been written on the role of the extended family among the middle classes than the working class. Willmott and Young, however, found that middle class families in Woodford kept up a great deal of contact with their families. 66% of the working class wives interviewed had seen their mother the previous week, and 62% of the middle class had done so. What is more, in Woodford where many working class couples were first generation settlers, grandparents often found it easier to maintain relationships over long distances because of their great mobility.

In fact 31% of the middle class wives in this sample lived within a radius of one mile of their parents. Two couples actually shared a house with the wife's parents, which means they met every day. In one wife's case her mother, a retired school teacher, looked after the children while the wife worked, which she did to support the family while her husband studied accountancy. In another case relations were more formal, but still 'we seem to bump into each other about three times a day'. 54% of the wives who lived within one mile of their parents, saw their mothers more than once a week. 'My parents are very old, and so I like to pop in once or twice a week,' said a sales clerk's wife. 'We seem to meet for some reason or other twice a week,' said a company director's wife, 'sometimes more often, but I talk to my mother every day on the phone.'

This is a very important point in making comparisons between working class and middle class extended family life, because by use of the telephone, middle class families can keep up contact over long distances.

27% of these wives met their mothers regularly once a week. The one remaining wife disliked her parents heartily and saw them as little as possible.

69% of the wives did not have their parents living nearby. 9% of these wives managed to meet their mothers at least once a week despite the fact that they lived outside London. 'We go down to Epsom for lunch on Sunday every week,' said a salesman's wife, 'because they don't tend to come up to London much.' For the others, 91% (62% of the total sample), contact was less frequent. In two cases both parents were dead, and the average contact for the rest was once every two months. One wife's parents lived in Bournemouth, and though they spoke on the phone a great deal, the family did not often go down to Bournemouth. 'But when we do,' she said, 'then we stay for at least three or four days.' A civil servant's wife's parents lived in Doncaster, and 'we never go there, but two or three times a year they come down and spend a week with us'.

This again indicates the difficulties of comparison. The middle class, on the whole, are more mobile and will overcome the problems of distance. The majority of wives who lived far from their parents were quite satisfied with contact by telephone and occasional 'stays'. Only 10% said they would like to have their parents nearby. In every case this was because they would like help with the children, either during the day, or for baby sitting at night.

23% of the wives had at least one sister living nearby, and 54% of these saw their sisters at least once a week. 'We were a close family,' said a manager's wife, 'and we are very used to seeing a lot of each other, it's a kind of habit.' 12% also had brothers nearby and 25% of these wives saw their brothers at least once a week. In one case this was because he lived in the same house as herself and her parents. A solicitor's wife always had her brother to supper once a week 'to make sure he gets a good meal inside him, he's a bachelor you see.'

Thus it can be seen that contact with parents and siblings is also quite common among middle class families. 33% of the husbands had parents living within two miles. 75% of these wives saw their parents-in-law at least once a week. 'My husband's father became very ill a little while ago,' said a teacher's wife, 'so now I look in every day. I can't say I enjoy it as he's a bad tempered old man but what can you do?' 'My mother-in-law is a great help with the children,' said a lecturer's wife, 'so I'm always dumping them on her as you might call it.' 'My mother-in-law never seems to be *out* of the house,' said an optician's wife. 'I expect its because it's her first grandchild.' 15% of the husbands' parents were now dead. This left 52% who were alive but did not live nearby. 28% of these wives saw their mothers-in-law regularly once a week, but for the majority, 72%, it was a case of two or three times a year. The husbands' siblings seemed more scattered than the wives' (and it should be remembered that 23% of the husbands had been only children). 17% of the husbands had at least one sister living nearby, 86% of the wives saw their sisters-in-law once a week. 23% of the husbands had at least one brother living nearby, and 55% of the wives saw their brothers-in-law once a week. In two cases the husband and brother were in partnership and contact between them was daily. The general impression gained was that the extended family certainly had a place in the lives of middle class families.

Ties between mother and daughter were obviously strong and contact by telephone often kept relationships flourishing and both sides in touch with each other's lives. But such relationships were not the central focus for the sample families, lives; and nor were they the main source of social intercourse. A great difference between the working and middle class wives was in the number and pattern of friendships.

Friends
67% of the wives said they had lots of friends. 'Hundreds,' said a company director's wife, 'literally hundreds.' And a great deal of time was spent in the company of these friends. 84% of these entertained friends at home regularly during the day and during the evening, and often went out with friends as well. 'We seem to have dozens of friends,' said a laboratory technician's wife, 'and we always seem to be visiting or being visited.' 8% of the wives mentioned that though they had a great many friends they tended to be separate from their husbands' friends and the two 'sets' usually remained apart. 'We tend to like quite different kinds of people,' said one, 'so we tolerate each other's friends and try to be nice to them when they come.' There was no wife who felt she had no friends, and the less sociable (33%) all said they had one or two good friends. 'I used to have many friends,' said an executive's wife, 'but now I've stopped work, it's less. I do have two good friends but they don't live as near as I'd like.' 'We have two or three couples we like, but no one living locally,' said another.

The general pattern of social life for these wives seemed to be a fair amount of entertaining and being entertained in the evenings, and a good deal of visiting of female friends during the day. Only 4% of the wives never visited a friend or were never visited by a friend during the day. One of these wives had been out at work until very recently and all her female friends were working too; and another didn't 'feel that sociable'.

This discussion of friendship is important as it serves to indicate how middle class wives were able to maintain a fair degree of independence outside their roles as mothers during the period when the children were young, while the working class wives were not. Yet as the study of work will show in the next section, the working class wife was just as determined as the middle class to work when her children were old enough, indicating that she did not see her role in society as that of a mother alone. In the middle class sample those wives who had joined the Housebound Wives Register were ones who had felt 'housebound' by their children, and thus had made an effort to do something about this with varying success. This was in fact more of a search for company in the day time than in the evenings. The evenings as the Newsons (1963) suggest are a time when middle class wives expect to be able to enjoy adult company.

Neighbours

The working class are the ones traditionally expected to be neighbour conscious and some of the earlier studies of moving into New Towns, such as *Family and Kinship in East London*, sought to explain the hostility between neighbours partly in terms of middle class attitudes which the working class had made their own.

In fact the middle class who, as suggested, have learned the necessary verbal and social skills required in getting to know new people, are probably better equipped to be neighbourly than the working class. In this sample exactly half the wives said they were on very good terms with at least one of their neighbours. 'I'm very friendly with one,' said a salesman's wife, 'and she often comes in to visit me.' 'She's my best friend,' said a television camera operator's wife of her right hand neighbour, 'though I must confess it took me some time to pluck up courage to knock on her door and suggest that her little boy came to play with mine. But now . . . well, I don't know what I'd do without her.'

Another 10% said they knew their neighbours but relations were rather formal. 'I talk to those with children if we meet in the street, but I can't say I'm good friends with any of my neighbours,' said a barrister's wife. 'They all made quite a fuss of me when I had the baby,' said a bank clerk's wife, 'but we're not really close.'

69% of the middle class sample had some kind of contact with their neighbours as compared to only 29% of the working class sample. Of those who had no contact with their neighbours all but three lived in flats. In fact 28% lived in flats or rooms, and all but one said that they had no contact with their neighbours, a confirmation of the difficulties for community living which flat dwelling presents. The one wife who lived in a flat and knew her neighbours, lived in a flat over a shop in an arcade along a busy road, and counted the shop owners as her neighbours.

In conclusion, it can be said that the picture of the social contacts enjoyed by the young middle class mother is one of a fair amount of activity in which family and friends play an important part. Physical contact between daughters and their mothers was less than in the working class sample, but contact by telephone was very frequent. As with the working class couple, the nuclear family was clearly the focus of the wife's attentions and interests, but she clearly felt the right to look to the world outside, whereas for the young working class wife it was an inward looking unit, from which contact with the outside world was considerably less frequent. (For example, 47% of the working class wives, all of whom lived within two miles of the West End, had not been there once in the previous year. Every single middle class wife had been to the West End within the last six months, although several lived right on the outskirts of London.)

Chapter Twelve

CHILDREN AND LEISURE

Going Out in the Evenings

The Newsons (1963) in their study emphasised class differences in patterns of going out. They found that middle class wives longed to go out, while working class women were content to stay at home. Thus in their sample 25% of Classes I and II never went out as compared to over 40% for Classes III, IV and V. The same disparity is revealed in this survey where wives were questioned as to how often they went out in the evenings. In fact only 4% of the wives never went out, which, considering that the majority had young children if not babies, indicates the importance of the evening to the middle class. A further 17% never went out with their husbands as there was no available source of baby sitting. 'We can't find anyone who's suitable,' said a lecturer's wife, 'so if there's a good film, then we just take it in turns.'

All the others, 79%, managed to go out together. Of these, 34% went out together more than once a week. Over half of these wives had living-in domestic help, three had tenants who baby-sat, and the rest used professional baby sitters. Friends, theatre and cinema were the most usual source of entertainments. One couple went gambling three nights a week, and another spent five evenings at a boys' club which they ran together. 50% of the couples who did go out together went out at least once a week. Again this was usually to visit friends or go to the cinema or theatre.

The remaining 15% managed to get out less regularly with the assistance of a relative or a baby sitter, going out whenever an opportunity arose. 'It works out at about once every two months,' said the laboratory technician's wife, 'if my mother comes to stay—then we can go out.'

Separate Outings in the Evenings

One indication of how closely the husband identifies with the restrictions of family life is the amount he goes out in the evenings without his wife. In fact 52% of the husbands in the sample never went out without their wives. 'He wouldn't go out without me,' said a teacher's wife, 'he would not enjoy it,' and this seemed to be the attitude of everyone else.

48% of the husbands did go out without their wives. Of these 26% went out regularly once a week to play bridge or squash or go to a club. 'I'm all for it,' said the barrister's wife, 'I think it does them good to get away, I don't see why a man should be tied to his home.' None of the wives whose husbands went out without them appeared to mind, whereas those who never went out separately appeared most emphatic that they would not approve of being left behind.

30% of the husbands who went out without their wives also baby sat for their wives regularly once a week. Thus one wife was able to go to evening class every Tuesday. 'I think I'd go mad if I didn't,' she said. The wife of a student accountant said, 'My husband doesn't like my friends, so once a week I take the opportunity of visiting the ones he doesn't like!' The remaining 44% went out occasionally if it was something special.

Certainly the general impression gained confirmed the Newsons' view that the evening is regarded as a period of activity and entertainment by middle class wives even at a time when their children are young.

Holidays

52% of the sample went for a holiday regularly every year

and 90% took their children with them. Most people went for an English seaside holiday and all were agreed that holidays were very important. 44% of the families were not able to take holidays regularly, but did so whenever they could. 'We've been three times to the sea in five years of marriage,' said the wife of a city clerk, 'the other two years something seemed to go wrong. But we shall go this year and take the baby!' 'We love holidays,' said a furniture designer's wife, 'but somehow we don't seem to get them regularly, but we went to Cornwall last year and the children loved it.' Only 4% of the couples never went on holidays. A bank clerk's wife said they were always too busy and an engineer's wife couldn't see the need for them.

Television

75% of the families possessed a television set and this undoubtedly provided a major source of leisure and entertainment. Only 17% of the families admitted to switching it on at least once every day but 58% said that if they were home in the evenings they usually watched. 'The trouble is,' said a teacher's wife, 'that though there are good things for grown-ups I disapprove of children watching so I never put it on when they are around.'

The question about television viewing was asked of middle class families in order to compare middle class evening activities with working class, for as will be seen in the section on working class leisure, television forms the principal source of leisure activity and entertainment for them in a way it does not for the middle class.

The middle class wives in this sample relied a great deal more on social intercourse with friends as a source of leisure than did the working class.

This section on leisure was aimed at discovering to what extent the children dominated their mothers' lives and to what extent they were still able to function as independent persons.

In conclusion for this section it can be said that it is once again clear that the middle class woman is able to retain a degree of free time for herself in the adult world, despite being the mother of young children. In a pamphlet called 'Women at Work', Anne Hopkinson (1961) wrote 'Women are seldom prepared for the worst effect of motherhood, that of cutting them off from all outside activities from which babies are barred and condemning them to the ... company of pre-school age children alone for the greater part of the day.' While probably most of the mothers would agree, some of the middle class mothers were clearly making every effort, not always successfully, to redress the balance.

PART II: WORKING CLASS

Going Out in the Evenings

Bennet Berger (1960) in a study of a working class suburb in the United States, noted that evening visiting between friends was not very common and visiting of any kind was rare except among relatives. Peter Willmott (1963) remarked of Dagenham that the main leisure activities were inside the home. This picture of a home centred family life among working class families is confirmed by this study.

44% of the wives never went out in the evening. Working class parents seem to mistrust 'professional' baby sitters and tend not to leave their children when young. As a driver's wife put it 'the answer is never, we've no family to leave the boy with, and I'd rather stay at home than leave him with a stranger.'

Of the 56% of wives who did go out 11% went out without their husbands. 'We take it in turns,' said a bricklayer's wife, 'to go to the pictures or visit the family.' But 90% of the wives who went out were able to go out with their husbands, though only 54% of them went out regularly once a week (27% of the total sample). For 73% of the working class wives it was go out together or stay in together. Only 27% of the husbands ever went out without their wives as compared to 48% of the middle class husbands. 'We'd both love to go out in the evenings once in a while,' said a railwayman's wife, 'but we've no one to look after the children, and there'd be no sense in us going separately as we'd not enjoy that.'

Certainly among these young families the 'absentee' father, thought at one time to be so common a working class phenomenon, now seems less common.

Details of Those Who Did Go Out
With one exception all the wives who did go out with their husbands made use of their families for babysitting. The one couple who did not were lucky enough to have a lodger they liked and trusted, and so 'We usually go to the pictures or a pub two or three times a week,' said the wife. Sometimes the children were taken over to a relative's house. The wife of a carpenter, for example, would visit her parents on Saturdays and they would put the children to bed at her parents' home, then go out to a cinema, and come back for the children afterwards. 'It works all right,' she said, 'though the kids get a bit cross at being woken up sometimes.' The cinema, pubs, and the dog tracks were the most usual form of entertainment, just visiting relatives was rare, this seemed to take place mainly in the day time, and visiting friends, as has been seen was also rare.

Only one couple in the whole sample still went dancing, although 81% of the wives mentioned it as their favourite activity before they were married.

Holidays
29% of the families never went on a holiday. The printer's wife didn't feel she'd enjoy them. 'Quite honestly the thought of taking the children to some strange boarding house, well it just doesn't seem right to us, though they get plenty of outings as we go scrambling every weekend.' But

the rest would have liked to go, but they felt that they could not afford it. But 50% of the families, and by no means all the most well off, took holidays regularly every year. 'We take a week at Maldon every year,' said a milkman's wife. 'I think the children must have a holiday to keep them healthy.' 'We go to Ireland for two weeks every year to visit my family,' said the wife of a motor mechanic, 'it's a holiday and I get a chance to be with Mum! We all love it.'

The remaining 20% took holidays when they could, but it did not always work out every year. 'I was expecting last year,' said a foreman's wife, 'so we thought it best to stay at home, but we shall take a week this year—I hope at Ventnor.' The seaside was definitely the most popular place for holidays. Several couples had been abroad before they had had children (all to Spain), but there were no couples who were planning to take their children abroad in the year of the interview.

Television

Television undoubtedly served as the main form of entertainment for practically all the families in the working class sample. Only one family did not have a television set—'the landlady won't allow it'—and this was one of the reasons for their desire to move. 79% said they watched every evening, and for many the television set was on all day from the moment the test card plus music began. Serials such as 'Coronation Street' appeared to be the most popular, followed by variety, plays and news. Many of the wives were not too keen on sport and complained that on Saturday afternoons their husbands sat glued to the set when they might have liked to go out. One wife felt this way about evenings too. 'The trouble is when he comes home in the evenings all he wants to do is watch television, he's tired, you see. Whereas for me, well I've been home all day and I'd like to go out. So you see television makes for arguments in this home.'

Zweig has suggested that the young working class man

has ceased to be involved with his trade union, his mates, his work, and these relationships have been replaced by the impersonal contacts provided by the mass media. This he argues accounts for the fragmentation of contemporary working class life, its loss of class solidarity, and the isolation of families. The evidence from this survey could be said to accord with this view. As has been seen the majority of husbands did not go out without their wives and this often meant they did not go out at all. Television provided them with entertainment within their own home, and as was seen in Chapter Eighteen many had few or no friends. However, it should be remembered that working class social life has traditionally been based on neighbours and the extended family and the degree to which this has altered is hard to estimate. Undoubtedly television was their main source of entertainment, and 50% of the sample watched a minimum of sixteen hours a week.

To summarise, it can be said that working class leisure is essentially home centred, with most activities taking place inside the home. There is far less effort than there is among middle class couples to keep up contacts with the outside world. From the point of view of the mother this means an almost complete submersion into domesticity with perhaps less opportunity for escape than her mother enjoyed, for whom at least there may have been an open front door and participation in some kind of street life.

Chapter Thirteen

MOTHERS AND WORK

PART I: MIDDLE CLASS

The history of women's work has been discussed in the first part of this study. At present there are approximately six million working of whom over half are married. (At the beginning of this century the majority of women who worked were single.) Many people have studied the reasons for married women to work, notably Viola Klein (1958, and most recently 1965), and the majority have concluded that financial motives were the most important. However, Viola Klein suggests that this financial motive is often one not of dire necessity, but rather to raise the standard of living of the family. Women, she goes on to say, are still dominated by the roles of wives and mothers, and go to work mainly as a result of reduced family responsibilities, not of a desire for emancipation. *New Society* (1963) quotes Sales Research Services on the results of a survey they conducted into the reasons for women working, which found the great majority, both of those who were working and those who were not, gave financial motives as the strongest reasons. (66% of full time working women, 54% of full time housewives.) Yudkin and Holme (1963) also found financial reasons the most important. F. J. W. Miller, S. D. Court, etc. (1960) said, 'we cannot escape the conclusion that the majority of women who went out to work did so because they were or felt they were under economic pressure.' The majority of these studies were mainly concerned with working class women, but in general it appears to be

107

accepted that in an affluent society acquisitiveness can be as strong a drive as sheer necessity. Women are equally spurred on to working, whether to feed the family better, or to pay for a holiday in Italy. Significantly the second most important reason given for working in the studies quoted above appears to be a combination of boredom and loneliness.

However, it is clear from a study of the educational background of the middle class wives in this sample, that they had envisaged work as something more than a financial aid and a solution to loneliness. For the great majority had trained to *be* something. 67% had stayed on at school until at least seventeen and 44% had gone on from school to some kind of full time further education, and 35% had done some full time training after leaving school. Only 10% had not been trained (or acquired training in a job) for some role other than that of wife or mother, and 77% of those who had trained intended to make use of their specific training when they returned to work. Of 22% who were not going to make use of their training, 33% were nurses, and they all explained this by saying that nursing was a twenty-four hour a day occupation, and did not lend itself to being carried out by someone who had outside interests or responsibilities. One ex-nurse, however, said that she enjoyed being a theatre sister so much, that if someone offered her this as a part-time job she would be very 'tempted'. However, all the ex-nurses were hoping to work in some capacity connected with public health.

This relationship between past training and future work intentions demonstrated by the women in this sample is in direct contradiction to the position taken up by Sir John Newsom in the *Observer* (1964). 'In the main,' he said, 'girls lack the ambition to acquire skills.'

Work before Marriage
The pattern of work for women today is to work till marriage, work after marriage, stop when the children are

young and return again when they grow older. This pattern is directly reflected by the women in this survey. All but 6% of the wives had worked before they were married. One wife had led an upper middle class adolescence of finishing schools and coming out dances, and had not really thought of working. 'I wish I had done something,' she said. 'I expect I'll have to do charity work if I am bored when the children grow up.' A company director's wife had married at eighteen, straight after leaving school. 'I regret sometimes that I didn't work or go to University, possibly I would have if I hadn't met my husband. Sometimes I feel as if my brain is disintegrating.' Another wife had also married at eighteen, and her South American husband had strong views on women working.

Work after Marriage

83% of the sample continued to work after marriage. Those who did not work after marriage included, it should be remembered, three who had never worked. Thus five wives actually ceased to work after they were married. Three were ex-nurses; two said, obviously they could not go on nursing after they were married, and by the time they'd started to look for something else they were pregnant. The third ex-nurse said her reason for not working was a combination of the difficulty of finding part-time nursing and opposition from her husband who needed to feel he was the 'bread-winner'. A store manager's wife said she became pregnant too quickly, and a city clerk's wife said she had been a nanny and was only too glad of 'a rest'.

The remaining 83% thus continued to work, although 23% of them changed from full to part time work.

Work after Birth of First Baby

The patterns of work changed distinctly after the arrival of the first baby. As has been said 10% of the sample had not worked after marriage. After the birth of the first baby the percentage of mothers who were not working rose from

10% to 62%. Only 37% of the sample continued working after they became mothers.

It is worth considering the twenty-two mothers, 46% of the total sample, who stopped working after their first child was born. They were all asked whether they had done any work since their first child had been born, and when the answer was no, they were then asked whether they would like to be working, and the answers to that question revealed the reasons for their decisions. In fact all the answers fell into one of five categories.

No help available	Work not suitable	Wrong to leave children	No desire to work	Husband said stay at home
32%	4%	41%	4%	18%

It can be seen that the main reasons were connected with the care of children. 41% of these mothers felt it would be wrong to leave their young children. 'You've got to put your children first when they are young,' said one. 'I feel I must be around at least till the children are three years old,' said another. 32% of the mothers would have liked to work in some capacity, but were unable to organise suitable help for the children. Only one out of the total was not working because she just didn't want to work ever again. 'Home's my place,' she said. 'I worked for a time before the child was born, but I'm happy it's over.' She was, however, an exception, and 75% of the 'at home' mothers would like to have been working. For example the wife of a lecturer thought it wrong to leave young children, but at the same time was 'terribly bored'. A representative's wife felt more or less the same. 'I get so restless,' she said, 'sitting here all day with a bottle.' The wife of a research assistant was not so much bored as lonely. 'It's being all by myself that gets me down,' she said. 'I have to force myself to go out and visit my mother or sister-in-law to cheer myself up.' The problem of lonely wives has been much discussed in recent years. Elaine Grande (1961) wrote in the *Observer* of the results of a radio programme on the subject. They were, she said, 'inundated' with letters, from lonely housewives, and their major complaint was that their role had no importance either to themselves or to the outside world.

'Being at home all day is terribly boring, frustrating and to my mind very *inferior*,' was one comment. Another said, 'Bored? I'm just fed up,' and another, 'I am haunted by a sense of wasted time.' And another, 'the suggestion that bored mothers can find the interests and intellectual stimulus they lack whilst knee deep in young children is arrant nonsense.' In fact *all* mothers in this sample who had worked after they were married said they were often bored at home, and a quarter complained of being lonely as well.

However, as had been said, 37% of the mothers had in fact worked since their children were born, and wives (44%) were working at the time of the interview. But only *one* mother was in regular full time employment. She was a school teacher. She left her children with an ex-health visitor and was quite happy with the arrangements. As she pointed out she had long holidays when she was at home, and even when working was home by 4.30. All the others were in part-time jobs, as were those who had worked but were not working now. Examples of the kinds of jobs taken are listed below:

Part-time teaching	6
Laboratory technician	1
Runs ballet class at home	1
Works in husband's pub over which they live	1
Part-time secretarial	3
Act on TV occasionally	2
Coaching at home	1
Look after children at home	1
Work in nursery school	1

From this table it can be seen that 24% of the mothers had found work they could do in their own homes—coach, run a ballet school, work in the pub, look after children. 37% of the mothers who were working had found part-time teaching jobs. All of them had clearly found work that lent itself to being part-time.

The Return to Work when the Children are Older

All the wives were asked whether they intended to work at any time in the future. Only 8% answered no. This included the three who had never worked, and one who was happy 'just to be at home'. Thus 92% said they intended to work when the children were older. Indeed it was quite clear that this was regarded in part as an automatic process. This accords with the findings of Veness (1962). 53% of her girls indicated they would return to work at some time during their lives and the majority felt no need to give reasons for doing so, it seemed a natural part of their lives. The return to work when children are older was also noted by Yudkin and Holme (1963) who found that out of their sample of 1,209 working mothers the largest proportion were aged 35–44. 77% of those intending to return to work, as stated above, were also going to make use of their training when they did return. 'I shall be back like a shot,' said the wife of an accountant. 'I can't stand housework, I loathe being tied down, it will be a pleasure!' 'Oh yes, I shall certainly work full time again,' said a laboratory technician's wife, 'when the children are older.' 'I shall go back to teaching as soon as my youngest child is at school full time,' said the wife of a teacher.

Reasons for Working, or Intending to Work

Because it was felt that the correct question with regard to work was 'why are you not working?' rather than 'why are you working?' no direct question on reasons *for* intended return to work was asked. However, an assessment of the replies to all the questions on work, which were fairly detailed, showed that everyone had in fact revealed her own attitude to work and these could be divided into the following three categories: (1) financial incentives, (2) emotional and intellectual satisfaction, (3) automatic—in the sense that it simply did not occur to some of the mothers to stay at home if they were not compelled to. The majority of earlier studies have all found financial reasons as the chief incentive. In fact 64% of this sample indicated finance was one of the most important considerations. But, and this is very interesting, only 8% of the mothers revealed financial considerations to be the *prime* motivation, *more* important than any other. The rest of those who revealed that finance was important also indicated another reason as well.

Finance alone	6%
Emotional and intellectual satisfaction alone	29%
'Automatic'	4%
Financial and emotional and intellectual satisfaction	25%
Emotional and intellectual satisfaction and 'automatic'	27%
No desire to work	8%

From these figures it can be seen that the largest group giving one reason only was those who sought intellectual and emotional satisfaction through their work. Such a person was the wife of a teacher who said, 'I need to feel I am using my brain, and putting my mind to serious problems.' It can be seen that 27% gave a combination of reasons indicating both a search for intellectual and emotional satisfaction, and a feeling that working was automatic. This may appear to be a slight contradiction, but there was a group of wives, who while clearly feeling that to work was automatic also acknowledged their need for work in the sense that if they were prevented from working at a later date they would then feel both deprived and trapped. 'I'm a teacher who has taken time off to bring up my own children,' said one. 'I haven't stopped working, merely made a short interval!'

Views of Husbands
Undoubtedly, as previous researchers such as Viola Klein have shown, for a wife to work she needs the support of her

husband. 27% of the husbands were in fact opposed to their wives working. (Four of these were husbands of the four wives who did not intend to work, so thus were in agreement with their wives.) In all the other cases, however, the wives were planning to return to work despite the opposition of their husbands. One wife said that provided she made it clear to her husband that her children would come first, she thought she could win him round. Another felt sure that in time the results of 'me stagnating' will make him change his mind. The wife of a furniture designer was prepared to put up with a certain amount of opposition because 'if I only work part-time he won't really have anything to grumble at.'

For the rest, however, the husbands were in complete accord with their wives' plans. In one or two cases, the husband was nagging his wife 'to organise her domestic situation', so that she need not wait to go back to teaching till the children were older. This accords with Viola Klein who found 60% of husbands approved of their wives working, and 29% did not. Yudkin and Holme found roughly the same proportions with 26% husbands in full support, 60% didn't mind, and 10% were opposed.

To summarise at this stage. Out of a total of 48 mothers only 8% were planning to remain at home when their children were at school full time. All the others, 92%, were intending to combine the roles of wife and mother with other activities. No one was forcing them out to work, the problem if anything was the other way round; those who felt that great difficulties were set in their path felt ill treated and deprived. It was not that the majority disliked their role as mother; the chief reason for staying at home when the children were small was that they were aware of the responsibilities of motherhood and were anxious to fulfil these responsibilities. Thus while the majority were as Viola Klein described her sample 'dominated by their roles as wives and mothers', this was more a short term than a permanent situation. Clearly motherhood was a role that all wished (indeed possibly felt it their duty) to enjoy and perform well. But few saw this as bringing their working life to a complete end.

PART II: WORKING CLASS

As was said in the summary of the working class wives' background, only 21% had been to grammar school, and 73% had left school at the statutory minimum age. Only 19% had gone on from school to do any further training of any kind. Two had begun to train as nurses, and then had given it up. The others had all gone to secretarial schools and had become shorthand typists. A further 29% had gone into jobs which led to the acquisition of some kind of skill. The kind of jobs ranged from filing clerk to cook in a canteen. Thus 48% of the working class wives had some clearly defined skill as compared to 90% of the middle class. The fact that less than half the working class mothers had any skill underlines the statement by the Industrial Training Council that the bulk of girls who left school in 1961 got no systematic training at all. Less than 20% in fact received any kind of training for more than one year. Viola Klein (1961) in her study of married women working noted how few were in skilled operations. The great majority worked in unskilled operations, and only 8% of the full time workers in the manufacturing industry were in skilled jobs. Thompson and Finlayson (1963) in their study of women who work in early motherhood found the largest numbers in unskilled or semi-skilled operations.

Work before Marriage

Only one woman out of the total sample of working class wives had not really worked before she was married. She had been very ill, and though she had left school at fifteen, her family had preferred her to stay at home and help with the rest of the children—there were eight of them. She did go out and clean for a month but had to give it up. As was said, 48% of the wives went into some kind of skilled work, 30% of these were shorthand typists and a further 35% were working in offices in a less skilled capacity. The remaining 35% of those with skills were in a variety of jobs ranging from telephonist to dress-maker. The other 52% of the sample had done unskilled work; 28% of these had been cleaners of one kind or another either in shops, factories or private homes. The remaining 72% had not stayed in any job for very long and had moved from one kind of unskilled work to another whenever they felt like a change. 'You got so bored doing the same old thing all the time,' said a carpenter's wife.

Work after Marriage
As with the middle class sample the great majority of wives continued to work after they were married. Only 10% in fact stopped working at marriage: three because they became pregnant 'too quickly' and two because their husbands forbade it. 'My husband needs to feel he's boss,' said one wife, 'and that means he must be the breadwinner.' 'I wanted to work,' said another, 'but he would not hear of it.' One wife had not really worked before marriage, so 87% of the sample continued working until they had children.

Work after Birth of First Baby
As with the middle class the patterns of work alter clearly after the birth of the first child, and the percentage of mothers not working rose from 12% after marriage to 71%. Only 29% of the sample continued working after they became mothers (as compared to 37% of the middle class sample).

If we consider the reasons for stopping work then similarities between the classes can be seen. Viola Klein (1958) found that among the non-workers the main reasons were husbands' opposition and fear for the children, which is true of the answers given by both classes in this study.

(as % of 28)

No help	Work not suitable	Wrong to leave children	No desire to work again	Husband forbids
7%	0	54%	11%	29%

54% of the mothers stopped working because of their obligations towards their children. 'I wouldn't want to leave them,' said a driver's wife, 'I'd miss so much.' 'I don't want to leave the children with just anyone,' said a postman's wife, 'though I can't say they are very exciting company.' 29% gave their husband's opposition as the main reason for their stoppage (as compared to 18% of the middle class). 'My husband expects me to stay at home until the children are at school,' said a motor mechanic's wife. 'He won't hear of my working,' said a groundsman's wife, 'and he's very stubborn about it.' 'It's his view,' said a removal man's wife, 'that a mother's place is with her children.' But whereas only one middle class wife had no desire to work once she had become a mother, 1% of the working class wives who stopped working gave this as their reason. 'I haven't time to think about work, I'm too busy,' said one, and another said, 'children are a full time job and the best sort of job there is.' As in the middle class sample, however, 68% of the 'at home wives' wished they were working (the figure was 75% for the middle class), and just like the middle class wives, many were bored and lonely at home. It has sometimes been implied that the conflicts of 'home versus work' are greatest for the educated middle class woman. This survey supports the point made by Thompson and Finlayson that the problems for all classes are becoming similar. 'The difficulties confronting a highly educated mother today may resemble those of a manual worker much more closely . . . than in the past.' In fact what has probably happened is that the now servantless middle class wives with young children are leading a life not dissimilar to that of many workers' wives. A report in 1917 by Janet M. Campbell on the Physical Welfare of

Mothers and Children noted that for the average working class woman 'her day begins, continues and ends with household drudgery, that the claims made on her time by husband and children are . . . unceasing, and that the better the mother the less the leisure.' Margery Spring-Rice (1939) wrote in the thirties that the working class mother is 'almost entirely cut off from contacts with the world outside her house. She eats, sleeps and "rests" on the scene of her labour and her labour is entirely solitary.' The rise of gadgets and the decrease of domestic servants during the century has not proved an entire blessing to the middle class wife who has found that housework tends to expand as the standard of living goes up, for example the acquisition of a washing machine may mean that sheets previously sent to the laundry will be washed at home, and the washing machine as yet does not iron them. As one correspondent of Elaine Grande's (1961) put it, 'I work twice as hard as my mother who had no washing machine but did have a maid.'

In fact the majority of wives, both working class and middle class, appear from the discussion of their own views on home and work to be essentially on the horns of a dilemma. They want to work, and feel curiously function-less when not working, but at the same time they sense their great responsibilities towards the children. In both groups those who were at home gave the children as their main reason for being there. A dress cutter's wife, for example, was very lonely. 'I'm used to an office with people coming and going, and now I don't get any company at all. I don't want to leave my children but I would like some company.' A labourer's wife just said, 'Some days I'm so fed up I could scream.' 'You've no idea,' said the wife of a plumber's mate, 'what it's like to spend all day in one room, trying to keep the children quiet because the landlady can't bear noise. I feel like I'm in a cage.'

If the fourteen mothers, 29% of the sample, who continued to work are considered in detail certain facts emerge. Not one of them had been in regular full time employment after having their first child. 36% of them had turned to regular part-time employment, which they were still pursuing at the time of the interview. A plasterer's wife worked as an usherette in the local cinema in the evenings only, so her husband looked after the children. A garage attendant's wife was a baby minder, and looked after another little boy in her own home all day. The wife of a groundsman went out cleaning and took her little girl with her. Two wives did have problems with the children, as they both worked part-time in offices. A printer's wife put her young child in a nursery one day a week, the older boy was already at school. The wife of a railway clerk left her two girls with her mother-in-law. The remaining 64% had all worked temporarily and given it up again, in each case stopping because of the children, either because they were unhappy or because the organisational problems were too great. A mechanic's wife, for example, found the cost of the nursery was over half what she was earning so 'it didn't seem worth the effort'.

The Return to Work when the Children are Older

As with the middle class wives the great majority intended to work when their children were older. Only 12% of wives did not intend to work again. This included the two whose husbands forbade it, and one wife who had been so ill that her health was in danger if she worked hard at caring for her own home. The others felt that the combination of their husbands' antagonism to their working, plus their own enjoyment of their homes, meant they would probably not work. 'Mind you,' said a textile worker's wife, 'I say this now, but come and see me in ten years' time and you might find I'd changed my mind.' But the great majority, 87%, were planning to return to work. The working class mothers were considerably less clear than the middle class as to what kind of work they would do. It will be remembered that 48% had some clearly defined skill. But only 65% of these intended to make use of this skill (that is 31%

of the sample). All the others wanted a change or didn't think they'd find the right sort of job. None of those who had worked in unskilled jobs were sure what they were going to do. This contrasts greatly with the middle class wives who clearly saw the whole question of work and home as being closely related to the specific job they wanted to do. With the working class wives the choice of the type of work done was clearly less important. However, it may also be that the choices for the working class women were more limited, partly by their own lack of training and partly by the attitudes of employers to the employment of married women. As Elizabeth Gundrey (1963) pointed out in the *Sunday Times*, women often encounter special discriminations when they are employed on a temporary basis and may be barred from superannuation. Indeed it seemed very likely that many of the wives in this sample saw no other alternative to cleaning or doing unskilled work in factories. In fact 33% of the wives expressed regret that they did not have any training of any kind, and several would have clearly welcomed the opportunity to remedy this. However, while society is slowly coming to acknowledge the right of the middle class woman to train in middle age (Birkbeck College, for example, had about twenty housewives amongst 1,000 evening students), the opportunities for working class women to do so are limited. This is despite the fact that many industries such as clothing, textiles, and the retail and distributive trades, are very dependent on female labour. As Stewart (1961) pointed out industry will become progressively shorter of workers as the number of unmarried women declines, and the shortage should be at least 200,000 by 1973. Nancy Sear pointed out that the employment of women in unskilled jobs cannot continue indefinitely as in many industries technological changes are reducing the amount of unskilled work available. Certainly the working class women of this sample, as much committed to working as the middle class, are going to be victims of this lack of opportunity.

Reasons for Working

The answer to this was obtained in the same way as for the middle class sample, and the answers fell into the same three categories—financial, emotional and intellectual.

	M.C. %	W.C. %
Finance alone	6	15
Emotional and intellectual satisfaction alone	29	10
Financial, emotional and intellectual satisfaction	25	29
Emotional, intellectual satisfaction and automatic	27	21
'Automatic'	4	8
Financial and 'automatic'	—	4
No desire to work	8	12

A look at the figures above reveals that finance is clearly a more important factor in motivation as might be expected amongst working class as opposed to middle class wives. 15% gave it as their sole reason as compared to 6% of the middle class. 'We could save for a house if I worked,' said the wife of a groundsman, 'and we've got to get out of this place sometime.' Only 10% of the working class wives gave intellectual and emotional satisfaction as the chief reason, but this difference may reflect class differences towards work in general. It would probably be true to say that the working class wives in this sample, destined for the less stimulating jobs saw work as a means of earning money, the middle class wives, however, tended to expect or hope for personal satisfaction from their work quite apart from financial gain. However, 29% of working class wives gave reasons for working which clearly indicated a combination of financial and emotional and intellectual reasons. A driver's wife, for example said, 'We need the money and I need the interests.' (She worked as an usherette.) And a lorry driver's wife said, 'Well it's the money, you know, and then again I feel I must *do* something.' 21% did not indicate money as the main incentive at all, but rather gave emotional reasons, while also indicating that a return to work was automatic once the children were at school. 'What could I do at home in this tiny flat?' asked a packer's wife. 'Once Garry's at school there's nothing to hold me here.' It appears, thus, that the attitudes of the working class women to working were not so very different from the middle class after all.

Views of Husbands

Thompson and Finlayson found that the number of husbands who did not want their wives to work increased as they descended the social scale. And in fact there were more disapproving husbands in the working class sample. (It must be taken into account that it is possible that the wives did not report their husbands' feelings accurately.) 40% of the husbands were opposed to their wives working, which meant that 27% of the wives were intending to work despite their husbands' views. 'I get so depressed,' said a packer's wife, 'that I'm willing to argue him round. What I do know is that I'm not sitting at home all day.' The wife of a despatch clerk felt the same. 'It's all very well for him to say stay at home when he doesn't have to!'

For the rest, however, their husbands completely approved of their plans, indicating that the majority of young husbands in the sample did not see their wives' roles in terms of domesticity alone.

To summarise, despite lack of education, lack of training and limited employment opportunities, the working class wives in this sample reveal work patterns very similar to the middle class. And this was also despite the fact that they appeared more dominated by their roles as wife and mother than were the middle class.

PART THREE

Conclusions and Proposals

Chapter Fourteen

CONFLICT AND AMBIVALENCE

As Nichols and May once put it, the role of woman today 'is incredibly ambivalent'. There is an air of confusion which hangs over the whole question of women and their functions in society which seems at times to extend to every aspect of their activities. First there is confusion over what precisely constitutes the psychology of the female. Carstairs (1964) in his Reith lectures, noted that surveys show a higher incidence of neurotic illness among women than men. This is in part, he suggests, because old ideas of what constitutes the feminine psyche such as those put forward by Earl Barnes (1912), 'Man creates, woman conserves, man composes, woman interprets, man generalises, woman particularises, . . . man thinks more than he feels, woman feels more than she thinks,' are in fact incompatible with the variety of roles she can now perform. The influence of Freud has probably played an important part here, offering, just at the time of woman's liberation, a rather rigid view of female psychology. In fact as Margaret Mead (1962) points out, we know very little about what constitutes the true psyche of the female. For example, the opinion is widely held, that to remain childless is for a woman to offend against her basic nature, and thus to do herself harm. However, we do not know to what extent being childless causes a woman harm, though obviously in a society which equates being a woman with motherhood there must be some effect. Yet even in this sort of society, nuns are not accused of doing themselves harm, because devoting oneself to God is socially acceptable.

Conclusions and Proposals

The confusion over what constitutes the essential psychology of the woman is extended to equal confusion about what constitutes her sexual role. Freud (1932) considered this to be in part a passive one. He also felt that the sexual instinct in women was less strong than in men. Yet our society is by no means certain that women have or indeed should have weaker sexual desires. Until very recently, a popular male view was to conceive of two types of women, virtuous and vicious. This was the accepted view in the nineteenth century and it was against just this type of mentality that Josephine Butler waged her campaign against the Contagious Diseases Act. The Act has long since been repealed but the ambivalence is still with us, although today the same respectable woman is often required to play both roles. Thus as Clifford Kirkpatrick (1955) says, women are asked to show restraint premaritally—the 'loose woman' is after all the subject of 'respectable scorn', but afterwards—in marriage she is expected to be ardent and uninhibited.

Underlying this ambivalence over sex is the question as to what are the essential differences between male and female. As Margaret Mead suggests, certain traits do appear to be fairly universal. In every known society whatever the principal male activity happens to be, it is regarded as of paramount importance. What is also true is that activities which are the sole preserve of man tend to be regarded as of more importance than those which are performed by either sex. Obviously there are certain undeniable differences between male and female springing from their biological inheritance. In Mead's opinion the most crucial of these is the onset of puberty and its aftermath, for the female this is unmistakable, and from then until the menopause the female is commited to a cyclic rhythm of existence. The male, for whom the onset of puberty is a gradual change, is committed to no such cyclic limitation, and as Mead says, 'Emphasis on the male work rhythm is an emphasis on infinite possibilities,' while for the female it is 'emphasis on a defined pattern of limitation.' However, beyond this we cannot go as yet, except to bear in mind that it is useless to consider the position of one sex in a vacuum. Graveson (1957) suggests that 'Women have succeeded in spite of their sex, instead of succeeding because of it, for they have generally based their claims to equal treatment with men on the superficial factors of similarity rather than the fundamental ones of dissimilarity.' Gorer (1961) neatly turned the tables on Freud by suggesting that the conflict between male and female drew its roots from the male seeking achievement in order to compensate for an inability to bear children. Thus the male searches for activities which can be his alone, and exerts pressures on the female to be a mother and nothing else.

This ambivalence over what constitutes the essential male, and what the essential female, must obviously have its impact on marriage patterns. We have seen from this survey that there is a surprising unity, as opposed to division, of labour in the homes of many of these young couples both working and middle class. In a sense many young women may be anticipating, in their patterns of marriage, a situation which does not yet exist in the wider context of society. At the same time for others marriage had, as an institution, proved a kind of trap. Some observers have commented how the young working class girl regards the build up to marriage as a golden period and sees marriage itself as a marvellous event, but does not really think beyond this. Probably the whole problem is aggravated by the tendency to oversell marriage as kind of unending affair, in which the partners are expected to remain at the high point of infatuation for the rest of their lives; and in this romantic picture there is no clear definition of what the roles and functions of the partners will be.

However, aside from the romantic attitudes towards marriage our society holds quite clear-cut views as to what constitutes the functions and tasks of a wife and mother. Today a woman is expected to run the house efficiently, higher standards of hygiene must be observed, but she must not be submerged by domesticity, which has definitely lost its sex appeal. This is confirmed by a poll by *Fortune*, quoted by Margaret Mead, which revealed that out of a choice of three pretty girls, the one most favoured by men as an ideal prospective wife was the one who had also been very successful in her job. Women today are considered to have two choices, to work or to stay at home. This implies that staying at home does not involve work. Yet at a time when the rest of the industrialised world is moving towards a forty hour week, women, many of whom may work at least eighty hours per week, are encouraged to regard this as not being work. In fact as Myrdal and Klein (1956) point out, 2,340 million hours are spent annually by housewives in Sweden on this 'non-work' while industry only uses 1,290 million hours. Domestic help is decreasing rapidly and in the last decade, says Elizabeth Gundrey (1963), domestic workers in this country have been reduced in numbers from 430,000 to 230,000. Gadgets have an inbuilt tendency towards Parkinson's Law. Sheets once sent to the laundry are now washed in the washing machine; curtains, blankets, etc., once allowed to get dirty must now be kept to the high standard concomitant with the possession of a washing machine. In a society in which leisure is coming increasingly to be prized, the housewife is left out. She does not even get paid overtime if she works in what is normally considered to be leisure times, Easter, Christmas, bank holidays. A report in Germany showed 14% of males interviewed to have had no holiday in the previous year; among women the figure was 63% and if only housewives were considered the figure was as high as 79%. A lot of housework is drudgery. Nothing has prepared young wives for the relentless boredom of scrubbing floors and ironing shirts. But on the other hand there is the feeling that being at home is not as important as being at work. Again as a correspondent said to Elaine Grande, 'Being at home all day is terribly boring, frustrating, and to my mind very *inferior*.' A correspondent in *The Times* (1961) complained in an article entitled 'Happy Though Married', that 'measured by the values of a society like ours where the real business of life is held to be what people do during their working hours I'm standing still. I don't exist.' For her, the non-existence which involved her saying, 'I keep house, look after a husband and children, shop, cook, clean (well in moderation), potter, read, write letters . . .' was exceedingly pleasant, for many it was torture. 'I'm haunted by a sense of wasted time,' said another of Elaine Grande's correspondents. 'Bored, I'm just fed up,' said another, and another said, 'A housewife does not merit the same respect as a woman who goes out to work, not even from her husband.' As has been seen in this survey the young wife's answer to coping with housework was in many cases to make her husband share it. But as one middle class wife said, 'he can share the housework as much as one likes, but he still walks out into a different world at half past nine every day.'

Nowhere perhaps are the conflicting ideologies which surround the role of the female in our society more clearly demonstrated than in her role as mother. As Yudkin and Holme (1963) say, 'It is a curious paradox that the growing emancipation of women and the gradual though uneven success of their claim to equal opportunity with men in undertaking various tasks in the community is coupled with almost universal acceptance that it is the mother who must carry the main burden of the responsibility for the care of the children.' There is also a curious duality about motherhood. For example in the eyes of the advertisers it is an extremely glamorous activity. 'Smiling mothers with enchanting babies' gleam at us from every sort of advertisement and magazine. At the same time reality is acknowledged by the view that if something does go wrong when the baby arrives it is of course entirely the fault of the mother. Here theories of maternal deprivation so valuable in their application to children in any form of institutional care have brought added pressure to bear on the mother. Margaret Mead (1954) has called these 'a new and subtle form of anti-feminism in which men—under the guise of exalting the importance of maternity are tying women more tightly to their children . . .' And Yudkin and Holme in their review of the available literature on the subject could find nothing to support the wilder statements about serious psychological trauma to the children whose mothers worked. We do not have any real evidence to support the view that mothers have *always* cared solely for their children. Indeed it may be that the mother of today spends more time with her children than did her mother, as she has no one to leave the children with. In fact the advent of children brings with it isolation, confusion and insecurity. The time when children are young, says a booklet issued by the Marriage Guidance Council (1963), is a time of 'pots and nappies, crying, feeding and the all important business of burping. It is the most extraordinary mixture of the sublime and the ridiculous, the anxious and the funny, and it goes on and on. This is perhaps the stage of life when men and women have to work harder than ever before or after-wards.'

It is also a time which involves a great loss of confidence to many a young woman. 'I felt such a failure as a mother not knowing whether the baby was warm enough, or fed enough, or why it was crying. I began to doubt that I could ever do anything properly again,' said one middle class wife. And another remarked that 'I felt, I was a failure as a person too,' and from this moment she began to feel lonely and isolated. In fact of Elaine Grande's lonely wives, the typical one was found to be 'almost without exception the mother of under school age children'.

This study has attempted to analyse some of the reasons behind the existence of the problems just restated above. The survey provided an opportunity to consider these problems in detail as they were reflected in the lives of the women in the sample. It is also worth considering the conclusions that can be drawn from the survey as they relate specifically to the women under study.

Chapter Fifteen

RESULTS OF THE SURVEY SUMMARISED

I. THE HOME

AS has been said, the quality of family life is greatly influenced by the standard and type of housing. The survey revealed no particular problem in housing, among the middle class. However, among the working class wives, quite apart from the generally bad level of housing, a specific point did emerge directly relevant to the problems of the young mother. This can be divided into two parts: (1) Who does she talk to? (2) Where do the children play? None of the wives in this sample engaged in the kind of 'street life' traditionally associated with working class urban life. As has been said, this depends on a stable population, familiar with the area and its inhabitants, a street level front door, reasonable safety from traffic, and perhaps most important of all a large number of home based women, available during the day. The young working class mother in this sample was confined to her home in a way that previous generations may not have been. The extension of employment amongst older married women, combined with changed urban conditions, has meant a fair degree of isolation for the mother with young children who has to be at home.

If street life gave the mother an opportunity for social intercourse, it also solved the problem of where the children played. But for the mothers in this sample to allow young children to play in the streets was considered very dangerous. And the children's play was a constant source of worry to 77% of the mothers involved in trying to keep their children under five happy in two rooms, possibly with neighbours underneath who were sensitive to noise.

Thus the absence of a 'woman's world' and a related street life has brought problems to the young working class mother, a problem of isolation, and a problem connected with the play of her children.

The middle class wives were not nearly so dominated by the limitations of bad housing. Many had gardens, and few were without somewhere for the children to play. Contact with friends and neighbours during the day also helped to ward off feelings of isolation, although the thirteen wives who were on the housebound wives' register had joined *specifically* to increase their social contacts.

However, housing as such did not present a specific problem to the middle class wife.

2. MARRIAGE

There is some evidence to support the view that the young working class wives went into marriage as quickly as possible, and that the marriage itself was not a sign of their acceptance of maturity, but an anti-adult gesture. 75% of the working class wives said that parental opposition to their marriages would not have worried or deterred them and 29% wives did get married against their parents' wishes. Only 42% of the middle class wives did not mind whether their parents approved of their marriage or not. Just 35% of the working class wives felt very strongly that they had married too young, and were now full of regrets for the things they had not done. The figure for the middle classes was 21%. It may be that the confusion surrounding women's roles affected their attitudes to marriage. For it was clear that for some wives of both classes marriage was seen as a kind of freedom; yet when it was combined with motherhood it became a kind of prison and they then felt their freedom had been restricted before they had really been free at all.

3. EQUALITY WITHIN MARRIAGE

The emancipation of women has undoubtedly resulted in some redistribution of power within marriage, but the question is how much?

Although legally the concept of 'marital unity' has been abandoned, the idea that in marriage the wife should submerge herself in her husband persists (she still takes his name after all). A story in *Woman's Journal* (1962) illustrates this point neatly. The heroine sought a career for herself and thus did not wish to marry. Eventually, however, she changed her mind and her prospective husband proclaimed joyously, 'Do you mean that you are no longer interested in belonging to yourself . . . Do you mean that you are interested in belonging to me?'

In this survey there were signs of a movement towards a fair degree of equality. Over half the wives of both classes felt their own relationship with their husband was more egalitarian than that between their parents; 56% of the working class and 64% of the middle class. But an interesting class difference was revealed. For the middle class equality meant *independence*, for the working class it meant *closeness*.

In conclusion the evidence from this sample on marriage reveals a fair degree of plain 'muddle' as to what marriage means and involves. However, these conflicts did not appear to express themselves in terms of conflict between the spouses. Rather the husband was enlisted as an ally against the institution of parenthood. In middle class terms, this meant helping to make the wife feel an independent person in her own right. In working class terms this meant fusing identities so that everything was shared.

4. CHILDREN

Class differences here were very important, so the relevant points will be made about each class separately.

Middle Class

1. Changes in patterns of family size meant that the majority of young mothers came from small families and 81% had had no previous experience of children or babies.

2. The impact of the birth of the first child on the young mothers in this sample was tremendous, because it changed them from being a new kind of woman to being the traditional woman. It meant in particular the loss of independence.

3. New patterns of equality were revealed in the degree to which the father participated in caring for the children.

4. The impact of modern theories of child rearing, and the great psychological importance of the child as a human being was revealed in the great degree of self-consciousness about child rearing. 62% felt their methods were better than their parents' because the children had a greater degree of freedom. But it was clear that the young mother felt a great burden of responsibility as a mother.

5. Attitudes to the education of the children reflected the women's attitudes to their own status. All were in favour of education, all but two most emphatically so, and only one made a distinction between the rights of boys to education and those of girls.

6. *Husbands*. The husbands in this sample shared many of the tasks of mothering. 44% would and did do everything for their children and a further 21% were rated as very helpful by their wives. The wives were very appreciative of this help and only one wife took it completely for granted.

7. *How Tied Down were They?* While 87% of wives worked until their first child was born, only 37% continued to do so afterwards. Thus in the majority of cases, motherhood,

if only temporarily, became the dominant role. 40% felt mothers should be with young children all the time. But only 8% of the wives were not intending to return to work when the youngest child was at school, indicating again the restriction imposed by motherhood.

Leisure, however, remained reasonably unrestricted; 67% of the wives went out at least once a week with their husbands.

In conclusion the young middle class mother of this sample felt herself to be carrying out a highly complex task in being a mother, but at the same time felt the need for some degree of independence. Some were more successful than others at achieving this, depending in particular on the attitudes of the husband and the availability of help with the children, either family, friends, domestic help, or nursery school.

Working Class
1. The use of birth control has never been so widespread as amongst the middle class, and many of the working class wives came from large familes.
2. To analyse the impact of the first child on the young working class mother is highly complex. The middle class wife took her role as a mother very self-consciously. The working class wives in this sample appeared to accept their role as mothers much more readily in theory, yet in fact were psychologically unprepared for the results. Their attitudes to and expectations of motherhood appeared to be derived from the old patterns of extended family street life. But the actual facts of their existence were a fair degree of isolation, reduced contacts with extended families, due to the difficulties of travelling with children, and loneliness through the contrast between their present existence as mothers and their previous existence as working wives.
3. The involvement of the working class father in the lives of his children was even greater than amongst the middle

classes, which may be due to the husband's awareness of his wife's problems, and a desire on his part to help. 62% of the husbands shared the children's care completely with their wives when they were home, and 27% were prepared to do almost everything as well. As in the middle classes, those wives whose husbands helped were extremely grateful for that help.

4. The impact of modern ideas about the importance of the way in which children are handled appeared to have had a great effect on the working class wives. 69% drew attention to differences in their attitudes towards their children from the way their parents handled them. As with the middle class, the young working class mother was aware of the gravity of her responsibilities.

5. Attitudes to education reflected the class differences in values placed upon it, and also revealed, despite the closeness and confusion of male and female roles with the nuclear family, a differentiation between the educational needs of boys and those of girls. 37% did not consider education important, and 19% said it was important for boys but less so for girls.

6. *How Tied Down were They?* While all the wives but one had worked regularly before marriage and over 87% after marriage, the majority as with the middle class stopped with the birth of the first child. Only 29% had attempted to work since this. Motherhood appeared to dominate their lives more than among the middle class. 79% felt that mothers should be with their young children all the time. (This may in part reflect the lack of available help in the form of nannies, nursery schools, etc. 76% of working class mothers said they would like to send their children to nursery school but few were doing so.) Leisure too was dominated by the family. 44% of the wives had not been out in the evenings since their first child was born. Only 27% of the wives went out regularly once a week with their husbands.

In conclusion the section on children reveals the working class mother to be dominated by her role as mother when the children are young. However, the great majority had worked before being mothers and intended to return to work, revealing that they did not see their entire lives in terms of fulfilling maternal roles and nothing else. It would appear that in the face of confusion the middle class mother was attempting to impose some pattern on her life over which she could maintain control, whereas the working class mother appeared to be blown with the wind, before marriage being completely work centred, then with children being completely mother centred. The future when she would work again was recognised but not coherently planned for. At the same time she was quite clear that she would work again when the children were at school.

5. *Organisation of Family Life*

Middle Class. Only one wife did not know her husband's income, all financial decisions were made jointly and 45% shared out the money without dividing it up into 'allowances'. Clearly the emancipation of women was reflected in the equal financial status of wife and husband.

A substantial minority of husbands, 21%, shared every task in the home and a further 44% regularly performed certain household jobs as a matter of routine. Again this may indicate a breakdown of the division of labour in the home. The family was a centre in which all the members were involved, it was no longer simply a 'woman's world'.

Working Class. 62% of the working class wives did not know their husbands' incomes. 94% shared financial decisions, but 77% kept strictly to a regular housekeeping allowance.

If the working class wife did not have quite the equality of financial status of the middle class, the housework was shared more exclusively among working class families. 54% of the husbands shared all the housework, and a further 25% would do anything if asked. This indicated the home centredness of the young working class family of this sample.

It also illustrated how the young mother was able to maintain some of the status she had previously when working, by obtaining her husband's help with the housework.

6. *Leisure*. In both samples leisure was mainly shared. 48% of the middle class husbands did not go out without their wives, and even fewer working class husbands did so; only 27%. Holidays too were either spent as a family unit or not taken at all.

The combination of lack of baby sitters and working class reservations about leaving children with anyone but a relative meant that the working class mother spent most of her leisure at home, usually in front of the television. Children restricted her leisure far more than they did that of the middle class mother.

7. *Social Contacts*. Both middle class and working class wives revealed close but not obsessive relationships with parents and kin. Few working class mothers had the kinds of relationships with their mothers of the kind described in *Family and Kinship in East London*, and in every case the centre of interest and loyalty was the nuclear family, which confirms for this sample the validity of the views set out in the Introduction. The young wife in this sample was not dominated by her mother, but she had also lost some assistance in caring for children that the old system provided.

Relationships with friends and neighbours were far more common among the middle class than working class wives, revealing once again how children tend to isolate the young working class mother from external social contacts. 25% of the working class wives had no friends at all as compared to none of the middle class. Many middle class wives felt that they were becoming rather isolated but they attempted to do something positive about it, such as joining the Housebound Wives' Register.

8. *Work*. 1. By means of education and training over 90% of the middle class wives had some clearly defined occupation by the time they became mothers and 77% of those

intended to return to the same kind of work when their children were older.

This reveals clearly that these women no longer saw their lives dominated in the long term by the role of wife and mother.

2. Only 19% of the working class wives had had any further education, but 29% had acquired some skill while working. Yet 87% were intending to return to work, and many would clearly work in unskilled jobs below their capacity. This indicates that roles of wife and mother had clearly affected their attitudes to training and work before marriage, a situation many now regretted.

3. 37% of the middle class mothers and 29% of the working class mothers continued to work when they had young children. The middle class wives arranged part-time work to fit in with the needs of their children, the working class were less successful at combining home and work.

4. The main reason for stopping in both cases was that it was wrong to leave the children. 68% of the working class wives who *were* at home would like to have been working, as would have 75% of the middle class wives who were not working.

5. The main reason for working among the middle class mothers was a combination of emotional and intellectual needs. The main reason for the working class was a combination of financial and emotional and intellectual needs. In both cases, however, the impression given was that the return to work was to some extent an automatic process. The *special* decision was the one to remain at home.

The conclusions, drawn from the interviews, reveal a remarkable similarity between middle and working class women in their patterns of work, and their attitudes to future work merely reflected class differences in attitudes to work as a whole.

Both samples were aware of the conflict over their roles as *mother* and *worker*. Neither saw clearly any great conflict between their roles as *wife* and as *worker*.

Chapter Sixteen

A FINAL ANALYSIS AND PROPOSALS FOR THE FUTURE

AS Viola Klein (1946) points out while women appear as citizens and workers on the front pages of our daily press, the advertising columns appeal specifically to their 'feminine emotions, her desire to please men by her looks and charm ... and her longing for romance'. This point is further developed by Margaret Mead (1962). There is, she argues, constant pressure on girls to play down and discipline an ambition that society at the same time continually stimulates. In Australia, as Norman McKenzie (1963) points out, the position is similar. 'From childhood onwards a girl is subject to a conflict of values. Marriage may be her main goal, but it is no longer an exclusive goal: before marriage, and increasingly at some point after marriage, she expects to play an independent economic role.' The resulting confusion led a correspondent in the *Sunday Times* (1963) to complain, 'Do today's women know *what* they want? They abandon a career in favour of marriage and children, and once having achieved both they don't seem to be able to wait to get back to work ...' The roots of this problem, suggest Myrdal and Klein (1956), lie partly in the fact that two views of women emerged in the nineteenth century; the lady of leisure for the middle classes, and the hardworking wife for the working classes, and today every woman is expected to combine the two. Also a legacy from the nineteenth century is the idea that it is basically evil to be a career woman, partly because it is always posed as a direct alternative to being at home, and many professional women feel compelled to state that they are not career women. Only recently has it come to be difficult to state emphatically that 'the role of the home maker cannot be shared, or that it is incompatible with external responsibilities'. However, the problems involved should not be underestimated. As a letter in *The Times* (1958) put it, 'If the new lady peer should arrive a little late for the debates it is to be hoped that the noble lords will not fuss. They were probably kept in, waiting for the window cleaner to finish, or the man to mend the vacuum cleaner or perhaps there were brussels sprouts to prepare for the evening meal.'

Clearly the nature of women's roles is changing, and the situation at present is one of conflict and stress. Nadel (1957) has suggested that all roles have one 'basic or pivotal' attribute which legitimises all the other aspects of that role. Now it appears that the central aspect of the female role is still conceived in terms of ascription; our society tends to respond to women for what they are rather than what they do. But this does not really become apparent until adult life, for as has been suggested, socialising processes both inside the family and more particularly in the school, allow and even stimulate some degree of orientation towards achievement. Girls are encouraged to do well at school in much the same way as are boys. So from the very beginning girls learn to develop aspects of their role which conflict directly with the base on which their role rests.

In fact the present situation could be summarised by saying that the 'problem' of women represents a network of conflicting roles which interact with each other, thereby aggravating the situation. At the centre of the network is 'Woman' about whose capabilities and responsibilities, conceptions and norms have radically altered in the last sixty years. Stretching out in different directions are woman's relationships with particular social institutions, and what is immediately apparent is that the value systems attached to these institutions often conflict directly with those attached to the roles women wish to play.

It has been seen how the ideologies that today surround parenthood conflict greatly with the values and expectations that women held before becoming parents. It has been noted that the set of ideas that support our present system of education which attempts to offer equal opportunity to all children to prepare for becoming instrumental members of a work orientated society, conflict considerably with the roles and functions of motherhood as conceived by the self-same society. The ideology of the modern family demands high standards of care, living and involvement which inevitably restrict the freedom that the 'new woman' has been encouraged to expect from her childhood and education. In the work situation many of the attitudes to women are again based firmly on past ideologies which ignore the realities of the present. As Nancy Seear (1964) said, 'We give women enormous responsibility as mothers and we reject them as managers. Why?'

The whole question was well illustrated in a different way by the Radcliffe College (Mass.) girl who asked Taya Zinkin (1963), 'What should I study so that whoever I marry I can continue to have an interesting and responsible job on a part-time basis so that I can look after the children without fear of growing stale?' This indicates, Taya Zinkin suggests, the pressure that all women feel, not simply the exceptionally talented, to reach outside their own homes.

'Men,' said one of Elaine Grande's (1961) correspondents, 'get the best out of life, for no one asks them to turn into house-husbands when they get married.'

Social change always creates problems, particularly by advancing more quickly on some fronts than others. But it does seem that some deliberate efforts could be made to ease the situation. *What is needed above all is some deliberate attempt to re-integrate women in all their many roles with the central activities of society.* A review of the general situation and a discussion of the specific points emerging from the survey indicate several ways in which this could be attempted.

We now have, both in public and private, an educational system that treats little boys and little girls very much alike. This is not because the educational system has been altered in spirit, but because girls have simply been absorbed into it. Our system of education was designed for boys, and it has been assumed that girls fit in well enough. And essentially the educational system into which women are expected to 'fit' is a class-based vocational system, created in the nineteenth century. At the higher levels it was aimed at turning the sons of the rising middle classes into 'gentlemen', and specifically it educated them to provide the professional and administrative class which the newly industrialised society needed. At the lower levels it was aimed at providing a new class of white collar workers, to staff the lower levels of the industrial society—clerks of every shape and kind. Education for the unskilled was not of primary importance, and skilled workers learned their skills through apprenticeships, *not* at school. Essentially this is the system we have today. The grammar schools have on the whole accepted the professional administrative ethos which the public schools created, and the secondary modern schools are vocationally minded without being quite sure what vocations to choose.

What is needed is:

a. A clear acknowledgement by schools that their girl pupils will be both working in the community and rearing children at various stages in their lives. Stress should be laid on the possibilities of combining these different roles. Pressure should not be put on girls to opt for one 'side' or the 'other'. They will probably regret it.

b. There is a clear need for improvement in the education of working class girls (as there is for the education of the working class as a whole). Many of the wives in the sample came too late to the realisation that they were capable of

144

working in a skilled job, and realising that they would not enjoy unskilled work.

c. Thus the education of women should be envisaged in three stages:

1. school
2. further education—leading to work
3. re-training for re-entry into work when the children are older.

This last should be a system of refresher courses, degree courses for mature students, and training courses of all kinds so that *working class* women who are going to work anyway *can* acquire a new skill or improve on an old one. It might also be useful to offer women the opportunity to take their degrees in two stages: the first part at the normal time, and the second part, as a preliminary to a return to work, after the children have grown up. The whole question of retraining is clearly going to be one of great importance for men and women as the rate of technical change increases, and it should be quite easy to integrate the 'mature' woman into this.

Apart from the obvious value to society as a whole of making use of its woman power, it would improve the psychological position of the mother at home if she knew that the paths back into work were clearly laid out.

A RE-ANALYSIS OF WOMEN'S ROLES AND CAPACITIES AS WORKERS

Essentially this means recognition by employers of the multiplicity of roles that women are called upon to play at various stages in their lives. It means on the one hand an acknowledgement that married women workers are a permanent part of our labour force, not just a temporary aberration. On the other hand it means making use of the full potential of women workers, and not regarding them as second class men. For example Nancy Seear (1964) found that there was 'fairly common agreement among the managers that women were unsuitable in line management'. But she could not find any comprehensive arguments to support this view. Most of the reasons given indicated that even where women were given the opportunity to perform instrumental roles, they were expected to show a strong bias towards expressive action *because they were women.* 'Women have emotional crises and can't take being kicked,' was a typical comment.

Firms who wish to employ women at that period of time when their responsibilities are greatest, will have to offer some system of part-time work. As a representative of one firm said to Elizabeth Gundrey (1963), 'Once the difficulties have been faced and overcome, financial and supervisory obstacles are not as impressive as they seem.' The subject of Women and Work has, by now been well discussed.

What is clearly needed is:

1. An extension in part-time work.
2. A close relationship between retraining schemes and work opportunities.
3. A reassessment by employers of the capabilities of female employees.

3. THE RE-INTEGRATION OF THE MOTHER WITH YOUNG CHILDREN INTO SOCIETY

Changes in the patterns of women's lives, and changes in the patterns of family relationships, which have been discussed both in general terms and with specific reference to the survey, have created a situation whereby the mother at home with young children is isolated from the main stream of society. In a work orientated society, those who do not work have some reduction in status, and housewives, no matter how arduous housework actually proves to be, do not feel themselves to be at work. At the same time there is no community of women whose lives have so many factors in common, and who share a common interest in the activities of the home. The nuclear family itself, as has been seen, is a focus of great interest to its members, and leisure activities are often performed by the nuclear family as a unit, rather than, for example, wives doing things with other wives, and husbands with other husbands. So the young mother today may not build up a network of relationships and activities with which to provide a central focus to her life.

One of the vital tasks for the future, the need for which this survey supports, is to provide some means of re-integrating mothers and young children into the central activities of society. Bracey (1964) in a recent study noted that American housewives suffer less from loneliness than do English housewives. The reason appeared to be that whereas children in America tended to bring mothers together for community activities, in this country the caring for children kept mothers apart. For example in the United States the Parent Teacher Association does a great deal towards integrating the mother into the community and providing her with the possibility of being instrumental in decisions which affect both her own children and the community at large. These kinds of organisations are less common here, although in recent years several have appeared such as that for the Advancement of State Education, or Mothercare for Children in Hospital, or the Pre-School Play Groups Association, all of which involve mothers and children in society. But how much these remain confined to the middle classes, and leave the working class mother uninvolved is not yet known.

There are three possible ways whereby positive efforts could be made to re-integrate the mother and young child into the central activities of society.

1. By the encouragement of such associations as are mentioned above, and also the official encouragement of Parent Teacher Associations along the lines experienced in America. The result would be to give mothers the opportunity to relate to each other, to the local community and

to society at large. This might go a long way to raising their status, as perceived by themselves.

2. By the improvement in facilities available for young children, particularly the under fives. More nursery schools, play centres and playgrounds would help to integrate the under fives into the community, instead of the present tendency to shut them away into their own homes.

3. By encouraging the community to include young children 'in'. This means making it possible for the mothers to live full lives and take the children everywhere with them. On a fairly mundane level this means making it easier to take children on public transport, for example providing more special places for putting push chairs, making it easier for children to be taken to self service stores, department stores, even art galleries, museums or adult education centres, in each case by providing supervised playrooms. Nursery school teachers should be able to bring their own children along. Health centres and baby clinics could employ mothers letting their children accompany them. Instead of children being excluded they should be expected and catered for.

By doing all these things society would be acknowledging the specific needs of mothers and young children. By including young children 'in', a situation would be created whereby life with young children would no longer be so utterly different from life without them, and motherhood would cease to be a kind of captivity.

It seems clear that the implementing of these proposals would make some headway towards resolving the conflicts in which many young mothers today find themselves involved. In particular it might mean that women could perform their traditional functions as mothers in ways that *complemented* rather than restricted their performance of other more contemporary roles.

APPENDICES
ON METHODS

I. DESIGN OF THE INTERVIEW

THE choice between alternative techniques of interviewing involves important issues of methodology—that is, it involves decisions about the type of information required, and the kind of analysis to which that information will be subjected. Interviews are usually classified on an unstructured-structured continuum, or unstandardised-standardised. The two extremes are on the one hand a completely formal interview in which the interviewer is merely a mechanical aid for the recording of the answers and on the other hand the informal interview in which the shape and form is determined by the individual respondent. The majority of interviews fall somewhere between these two extremes. Undoubtedly the more standardised the interview the more easily can the information be coded and analysed, and possibly most important of all, the more easily can it be empirically tested in the future by other researchers. However there are several disadvantages to this kind of formalised interviewing. It is, for example, not always desirable to present the results of empirical research in purely statistical forms. As Grebenik and Moser (1962) point out 'verbal descriptions of individual cases, institutions and the like can often give a more vivid, richer and in a sense, deeper picture of life than the statistical tables to be found in conventional survey reports'. This view is confirmed by Young and Willmott (1957) who found that while formal interviews could provide precise quantitative data within a limited range, the intensive interviews often provided richer material. Merton's development of the focused interview is in some ways an attempt to get the best of both kinds of interviewing. In this the interview has a fixed framework of questions, yet allows the interviewer a certain latitude within it. The main value of this type of interview, Merton (1946) suggests, is that it gives the respondent the opportunity to express himself on matters of significance to him rather than those presumed important to the interviewer. In fact many of the recent empirical studies of the family in this country have employed interviewing techniques which are variations on this theme. For in this type of study, the main object as Jennings (1962) suggests is 'to see the situation from the point of view of the person interviewed . . . The fact that in a few instances the narratives were highly charged with emotion and that such emotions were sometimes coincident with ignorance of the real facts of the situation did not seem to us to diminish their value.'

Without question the main disadvantage of this type of flexible interviewing is one of bias. A great deal of work has been done in recent years on this subject and there is now ample evidence to show that active commitment to a particular point of view during the interview considerably affects the results. In fact, Hyman (1954) at the National Opinion Research Centre found that it was precisely the expectations and attitudes of the interviewer which most influenced the responses given. Eysenck (1953) has also noted that where questions of opinion are asked the result may be a combination of both the interviewers' and the respondents' views. On the other hand, it is easy to overstate the problem of interviewer bias. As Sellitz and Jahoda, etc. (1962) point out, 'Much of what we call interviewer bias can more correctly be described as interviewer *differences*, which are inherent in the fact that interviewers are human beings and not machines . . .' After all, as they note, social scientists are universally dependent on data that have been collected by means of oral or written reports and these are 'invariably subject to essentially the same sources of error and bias as are those collected by survey interviewers'. Koos (1946) in *Families in Trouble* demonstrated how important it was, if the interview was to yield anything beyond the superficial, for there to be a degree of rapport between the interviewer and respondent. As every interviewer is probably aware, the problem can sometimes be to get the respondent to talk at all. Cannell and Kahn (1954) give two main reasons for respondents being 'motivated' to talk.

1. As has been demonstrated in experiments with small groups 'a person will communicate in a given situation if he believes that such communication will bring about a change or effect an action which he considers desirable'.
2. What can be called the 'therapeutic' motive. That is 'an individual is motivated to communicate with another when he

receives gratification from the communication process and the personal relationship'.

Essentially, they go on to say 'optimum communication takes place if the respondent perceives the interviewer as one who is likely to understand and accept his basic situation'. If this view is accepted as correct, then, at least at the beginning of the interview, some kind of commitment on the part of the interviewer is essential, and in fact this ties in precisely with the experience in this research. Probably, as Cannell and Kahn suggest, the ideal relationship between the interviewer and respondent 'seems to be one in which the interviewer achieves a considerable degree of closeness in terms of understanding and acceptance, but at the same time retains the detachment or objectivity . . . which we associated with a professional client relationship'.

It was with precisely this aim in view that the choice of technique for this study, which was concerned above all to discover the respondents' *own* perceptions of their situation, was made in favour of a fairly unstructured interview involving the flexible use of a schedule.

THE SCHEDULE

To some extent, every study is only as good as the questions it asks, and the problems of schedule design are legion, though they have been well documented.

The main functions of any questionnaire or schedule as Cannell and Kahn point out are on the one hand to translate the research objectives into specific questions, and on the other, to assist the interviewer in motivating the respondent to communicate the required information. In order to achieve both these ends it is vital that the questions should be cast in the language of the respondent. Thus there are two basic decisions to be made: First what questions to ask. This involves the definition of the problem to be studied and a breaking down of the whole into its relevant parts. The second decision is how to phrase the questions, which involves an understanding of the situation of the respondent, and of his expectations and limitations. Kornhauser and Sheatsley (1962) have compiled a guide list for formulating questions, which is extremely useful for avoiding the usual pitfalls of ambiguity, bias, complexity, vagueness, emotional content, etc.

Appendices on Methods

The aim of this survey was to build up a picture of the lives of the women studied, as they were at that very moment, which could be rounded out a little by their own recollections of their past, and their aspirations for the future. In order to translate this into a series of questions, the responses to which would build up this picture, a pilot study was undertaken. The subject was broken down into nine areas or topics (a system similar to that employed by Bott (1957) and Mogey (1956)), these being 1. The Home. 2. General Background of Wife. 3. General Background of Husband. 4. The Marriage. 5. The Children. 6. Organisation of Family Life. 7. Leisure. 8. Social Contacts. 9. Work. The interview was quite unstructured, these 'topics' being the only guide to the information needed. Every attempt was made to let the interview develop naturally, allowing the respondent to flit from one subject to another as often happens in ordinary conversation. Following Merton's advice any question from the respondent was countered with another one, thus, as he said, 'converting the implied content of the informant's question into a cue for further discussion'. Notes were taken during the interview, and the material was broken down afterwards into detailed sections under the appropriate headings. On the basis of material from fifteen interviews conducted in this way, the schedule was drawn up.

INTERVIEWING FOR THIS STUDY

Whereas in the pilot study the interview had been as unstructured as possible, this was not entirely true of the actual interviews for the research itself. The schedule contained a series of questions for which answers had to be obtained. A number of these were simple factual ones—how many rooms do you have—how many children do you have—and involved straightforward questions and answers along the lines of the more formal type of interviewing. At the same time experience in the pilot study had revealed two things. Firstly that a considerable degree of rapport was necessary for a satisfactory interview on this subject (which involved attitudes and emotions as well as facts), and secondly that if the respondent was allowed to follow her own train of thought, many questions would be answered without the necessity of asking them specifically, although in some cases it might be valuable to check back later. For these reasons some time was spent at the beginning of each interview establishing a kind of relationship by exchanging small pieces of conversational information. Once some degree of rapport had been established the conversation ceased, leaving the respondent confident and at ease, and allowing the interview to develop along the lines Merton suggested.

1. In an interview guidance and direction from the interviewer should be at a minimum.
2. The subject's definition of the situation should find full and specific expression.
3. The interview should bring out the value laden implications of response.

Obviously interviewing from the basis of a schedule could not be quite as 'non-directive' as Merton intended. However, as in the pilot study, each interview was allowed to develop naturally, enabling the respondent to direct the conversation along her own lines and filling in the schedule to suit her own order. This meant that the answers to many questions were obtained without any direct demand. For example every wife said something about her methods of bringing up her children. This was recorded in the appropriate section of the schedule, and *then* she was asked whether she found any difference between her own ideas and those of her husband, and those of her parents. In this way identical schedules were obtained from each person, which could then be compared, but at the same time each woman interviewed had been given a fair degree of freedom to express her own views in her own way.

To some extent being one's own interviewer both increases and decreases the difficulties. There is no problem of misunderstanding or misinterpretation of the schedule, nor of different questions being given varying importance. Any bias is constant throughout so that the schedules, when complete, have a degree of uniformity. The main disadvantage, however, is that if the interviewer is also the author of the research, as in this case, the very expectations that led to the promotion of the research may determine some of the responses given—along the lines demonstrated by Hyman (1954). It is difficult to see how this can be avoided completely, but awareness of the problem plus constant self control can help. In circumstances such as these, it is probably best to employ the kind of 'non-directive' interviewing that has been used in this research.

II. SCHEDULE

IT will be noted that this Schedule contains both direct questions and 'Summaries'. For an explanation of this see Appendix I.

I. COMPOSITION OF HOUSEHOLD

1. Number in household.
2. Extra from immediate family.

2. DESCRIPTION OF HOME

1. (a) Terrace; (b) Semi-detached; (c) Detached; (d) House; (e) Flat; (f) Furnished; (g) Unfurnished; (h) L.C.C.; (i) Council; (j) Private; (k) Self.
2. Length lived there.
3. Rent.
4. Number of rooms.
5. Children sleep: (a) with parents; (b) separately.
6. Amenities: (a) sep. dining room; (b) sep. sitting room; (c) own bathroom; (d) shared bathroom; (e) no bathroom; (f) own lavatory; (g) shared lavatory; (h) garden.
7. Would you like to move: (a) yes; (b) no.
   Reasons.
8. General description of home.

3. GENERAL BACKGROUND: WIFE

1. Age.
2. Born: (a) London; (b) St. Pancras; (c) England; (d) other.
3. Educated: (a) elementary; (b) secondary modern; (c) grammar; (d) private.
4. Age left.
5. Size family.

6. Parents alive.
7. Born: (a) London; (b) St. Pancras; (c) England; (d) other.
8. Now living.
9. Occupation of father.
10. Social Class of father.
11. Enjoyed years between school and marriage: (a) yes; (b) no. Reasons.
12. General comments on parents.

HUSBAND

1. Age.
2. Born: (a) London; (b) St. Pancras; (c) England; (d) other.
3. Educated: (a) elementary; (b) secondary modern; (c) grammar; (d) private.
4. Age left.
5. Parents alive.
6. Born: (a) London; (b) St. Pancras; (c) England; (d) other.
7. Now living.
8. Occupation of father.
9. Social Class.
10. Occupation of husband.
11. Wage.
12. Social Class.
13. Enjoyed period between school and marriage: (a) yes; (b) no.
14. Comment on parents.

4. MARRIAGE

1. Length.
2. Where did you meet?
3. Length of courtship.
4. Parental attitudes.
5. How important was your parents' opinion to you?
6. Age at marriage: wife; husband.
7. Do you think this was the: (a) right age? (b) too young? Reasons.
8. Did you want to get married very much before you met your husband?
9. General comments on marriage.

10. General comments on husband.
11. Comparison with parents.

5. CHILDREN

1. Number.
2. Complete.
3. Planned.
4. Where confined: (a) who helped with children.
5. Previous experience with children.
6. Does he help with the children? Would he for example: (a) walks? (b) feeds? (c) get up at night? (d) wash nappies? (e) change nappies? If none of these, what will he do?
7. General methods of upbringing: (a) self; (b) husband; (c) comparison with parents.
8. Do you think it important for children to be with their mother: (a) all the time? (b) most of the time? (c) not of importance?
9. Education important? (a) boy; (b) girl; (c) both; (d) not important.
10. Is this your view?
11. Does your husband agree?
12. Do you think your children are having a better childhood than you did?
   Reasons.
13. Do you find this home suitable for children?
   Reasons.
14. Would you like a garden?
15. What else do you think would be useful with small children?
16. If there were free day nurseries would you use them: (a) from what age? (b) for how long?
17. If there were more free nursery schools available, would you use them: (a) from what age?
18. What do you think is the best age to start school?

6. ORGANISATION OF FAMILY LIFE

1. Do you know your husband's wage?
2. How do you divide it: (a) you take it all and husband keeps pocket money; (b) husband gives you an allowance; (c) you share it?

3. Who makes the financial decisions?
4. If you wanted a washing machine, would you: (a) ask your husband to buy it? (b) save for it yourself? (c) save for it jointly?
5. Does your husband help with the housework? (a) if yes, would he do: (1) cleaning? (2) washing? (3) ironing? (4) washing up? (5) shopping? (b) if no, why not?
6. Is it the same amongst most of your friends?
7. How does your husband compare with your father? (a) helps more; (b) helps less.

7. LEISURE

1. Does your husband ever go out without you? (a) If yes, how often? (b) if no, why not?
2. Do you go out in the evenings: (a) how often? (b) where?
3. Do you go out at the week-ends: (a) how often; (b) where?
4. Do you take holidays: (a) how long? (b) where?
5. Do you ever go to the West End?
6. Do you watch television? (a) every evening; (b) most evenings; (c) sometimes; (d) not often.
7. What do you like best?
8. Do you listen to the radio? (a) a lot; (b) sometimes; (c) no.
9. What do you like best?
10. Do you do your own decorations? (a) your husband by himself; (b) together.

8. SOCIAL CONTACTS

1. Do your parents live near?
2. See them: (a) more than once a week; (b) once a week; (c) once a month; (d) rarely.
3. Would you like to see them: (a) more? (b) less?
4. Do your sisters/brothers live near?
5. Do you see them: (a) more than once a week? (b) once a week? (c) once a month? (d) rarely?
6. Would you like to see them: (a) more? (b) less?
7. Do your husband's parents live near?
8. Do you see them: (a) more than once a week? (b) once a week? (c) once a month? (d) rarely?

9. Would you like to see them: (a) more? (b) less?
10. Do your husband's sisters/brothers live near?
11. Do you see them: (a) more than once a week? (b) once a week? (c) once a month? (d) rarely?
12. Would you like to see them: (a) more? (b) less?
13. Do you have friends? (a) many; (b) few; (c) none.
14. Are you friendly with your neighbours?
15. Would you invite your neighbours in for a cup of tea?
16. Do you entertain your friends: (a) day? (b) evenings?
17. Do you entertain your husband's friends: (a) day? (b) evenings?
18. Do you entertain joint friends: (a) day? (b) evenings?
19. Do you ever go out with friends: (a) evenings? (b) week-ends? (c) holidays?
20. Did you do this before you were married?

9. WOMAN'S WORK

1. Did you work before you were married?
2. Did you enjoy it?
3. Did you work after you were married?
4. Did you enjoy it?
5. Why did you stop?
6. Have you worked since your children were born? If yes, (a) what kind of work? If no, (b) have you any desire to return?
7. Does you husband have the same views as you?
8. Do you find yourself bored at home?
9. Do you think your children would suffer if you went back?
10. Do you have any training? If yes, (a) will you use it? If no, (b) do you wish you had some?
11. What kind of job will you take if you go back?
12. Ideally what would you like?
13. If not going to work again, what are your feelings about work?

III. SELECTION OF THE SAMPLES[1]

THE working class wives were all drawn from the practice lists of the Caversham Centre, a Group Practice in Kentish Town. The files of the practice were arranged in alphabetical order, families together, and as these files were in constant use, any elaborate method of sampling would have been difficult. Selection was made as follows. An alphabetical list was taken from the files of all the wives who fell into the right categories, that is, (a) married, (b) at least one child under five, (c) born in or after 1930. Seventy were selected at random from the list, but twenty had to be eliminated as being ineligible. The method of approach was to call at the address, explain my introduction from the doctor, and ask if they would be willing to assist in the work. In fact two refused and forty-eight agreed. In twenty cases I was invited straight in, in the other twenty-eight another appointment was made. In nine of these cases, it involved yet another call before the interview took place.

SELECTION OF THE MIDDLE CLASS SAMPLE

Selection of forty-eight middle class women proved more difficult. The practice at the Caversham Centre had very few middle class patients, and the doctors felt they were not in any way representative of the middle classes in general. It was decided that the advantages of an introduction such as the one obtained at the Caversham Centre were sufficiently great to try to repeat this with the middle class sample. However, it proved very difficult to find a doctor who had a large number of middle class patients in the right categories, and who was willing to assist in the research. Advice was sought from the College of General Practitioners, and one doctor in West Hampstead offered to assist.

[1] The survey was carried out during 1960–61.

In fact a study of his files revealed only thirty-five names which fulfilled all the right conditions. An initial introduction to the thirty-five women selected was obtained through a letter from the doctor explaining the purpose of my research. Subsequently I telephoned to ask their assistance and arrange a visit. In no case was there a refusal. The remaining thirteen were selected from the London lists of the 'Housebound Wives' Register. This is an informal association, begun after a letter in *The Guardian*, of women with children. It has groups all over the country and discussion with the area organiser in North London revealed that its membership covered a wide variety of people. It is fully realised that to select from an organisation such as this involves a degree of bias, mainly due to the fact that the women have selected themselves, i.e. joined the group, and that this bias is probably a greater one than that incurred by selecting from a doctor's practice. However, the following points should be made:

1. The number was small.
2. The great importance to the success of the interviewing of some kind of introduction—this is reflected in the very low refusal rates, only two unavailable out of fifty working class mothers. *None* out of forty-eight middle class mothers.
3. It had been decided at the outset that the aim of the study would be a qualitative rather than quantitative presentation.

In fact it was anticipated that there might be some chances of bias in the working class sample due to the specific character of the Caversham Centre, which it was thought might attract patients with psychiatric problems. However, studies by Kessel and Shepherd (1962) and Kessel (1960) revealed no evidence of any bias on this or any other score.

BIBLIOGRAPHY

M. ABRAMS, 'The Home Centred Society.' *The Listener,* Vol. LXII, No. 1600. 1959.

M. ABRAMS, *Teenage Consumer Spending in 1959,* Pt. II. L.P.E. Ltd. 1961.

N. ANDERSON, *The Urban Community.* Routledge & Kegan Paul. 1960.

J. A. BANKS, *Prosperity and Parenthood.* Routledge & Kegan Paul. 1954.

E. BARNES, *Woman in Modern Society.* Cassell. 1912.

B. BERGER, *Working Class Suburb.* University of California Press, Los Angeles. 1960.

C. BOOTH, *Life and Labour of the People in London.* Macmillan & Co. 1903.

E. BOTT, *Family and Social Network.* Tavistock Publications. 1957.

J. BOWLBY, *Maternal Care and Mental Health.* W.H.O. Series 2. Geneva. 1951.

H. E. BRACEY, *Neighbours.* Routledge & Kegan Paul. 1964.

U. BRONFENBRENNER, 'Socialisation and Social Class through Time and Space.' From: E. E. Maccoby, T. M. Newcomb, E. L. Hartley (Eds.), *Readings in Social Psychology.* Henry Holt, New York. 1958.

N. R. BUTLER and D. G. BONHAM, *Perinatal Mortality.* National Birthday Trust Fund. E. S. Livingstone. 1963.

J. M. CAMPBELL, *Report on the Physical Welfare of Mothers and Children.* Carnegie United Kingdom Trust. 1917.

C. F. CANNELL and R. L. KAHN, 'The Collection of Data by Interviewing.' From: L. Festinger and D. Katz (Eds.), *Research Methods in the Behavioural Sciences.* Staples Press. 1954.

G. M. CARSTAIRS, *This Island Now.* Penguin. 1964.

F. LE-GROS CLARK, *The Economic Rights of Women.* Eleanor Rathbone Memorial Lecture, Liverpool University Press. 1963.

COMMITTEE ON HIGHER EDUCATION, *Higher Education* (The Robbins Report), Appendix I, 'The Demand for Places in Higher Education.' H.M.S.O. 1963.

N. DENNIS, F. HENRIQUES and C. N. SLAUGHTER, *Coal is Our Life*. Eyre & Spottiswoode. 1956.

D. V. DONNISON, C. COCKBURN and T. CORLETT, *Housing Since the Rent Act*. Occasional Papers in Social Administration. Codicote Press. 1961.

F. DOTSON, 'Voluntary Associations among Urban Working Class Families.' *American Sociological Review*, Vol. 16, No. 5, Oct. 1951.

J. W. B. DOUGLAS, *The Home and the School*. MacGibbon & Kee. 1964.

J. W. B. DOUGLAS, 'The Feminists Mop up.' *The Economist*, Vol. 179, No. 5879. 1956.

M. L. EYLES, *The Woman in the Little House*. Grant Richards. 1922.

H. J. EYSENCK, *Uses and Abuses of Psychology*. Pelican Books. 1953.

D. FIELD and D. NEILL, *A Survey of New Housing Estates in Belfast*. Queens University of Belfast. 1957.

R. FLETCHER. *The Family and Marriage*. Penguin Special. 1962.

S. FREUD. *New Introductory Lectures on Psycho-analysis and other works*. Hogarth Press and the Institute of Psycho-Analysis. 1964.

S. FREUD, *Civilisations and its Discontents*. The Hogarth Press and the Institute of Psycho-Analysis. 1957.

T. R. FYVEL, *The Insecure Offenders*. Chatto & Windus. 1961.

D. GEORGE, *England in Transition*. George Routledge & Sons. 1931.

D. V. GLASS, 'Education.' In: M. Ginsburg (Ed.), *Law and Public Opinion in England in the Twentieth Century*. Stevens & Sons. 1959.

G. GORER, 'Fifty Years After.' *The Observer*. 13th August 1961.

E. GRANDE, 'Lonely Wives.' *The Observer*. 11th May 1961.

R. H. GRAVESON and F. R. CRANE (Eds.), *A Century of Family Law*. Sweet & Maxwell. 1957.

E. GREBENIK and C. A. MOSER, 'Statistical Surveys.' In: A. T. Welford, M. Argyle, D. V. Glass, J. N. Morris (Eds.), *Society. Problems and Methods of Study*. Routledge & Kegan Paul. 1962.

J. GREVE, 'The Homeless Londoners.' *New Society*, Vol. 1, No. 8. 1962.

E. GUNDREY, 'Breaking out of Purdah.' *The Sunday Times*. 21st July 1963.

E. GUNDREY, 'The Way Back to Work.' *The Sunday Times*. 28th July 1963.

Bibliography

A. M. HAMILTON, 'Changes in Social Life.' From: R. Strachey (Ed.) *Our Freedom and its Results*. Hogarth Press. 1936.

A. HARVEY, 'Gaps in the Welfare State.' *The Observer*. 11th February 1962.

H. HIMMELWEIT, 'Social Status and Secondary Education since the 1944 Act.' In: D. V. Glass (Ed.), *Social Mobility in Britain*. Routledge & Kegan Paul. 1964.

R. HOGGART, *The Uses of Literacy*. Chatto & Windus. 1959.

A. HOPKINSON, *Women at Work*. Industrial Christian Fellowship. 1961.

J. HUBBACK, *Wives Who Went to College*. Heinemann. 1957.

H. H. HYMAN, *Interviewing in Social Research*. University of Chicago Press, Chicago. 1954.

H. H. HYMAN, 'The Value Systems of Different Classes.' In: R. Bendix and S. M. Lipset (Eds.), *Class Status and Power*. Routledge & Kegan Paul. 1953.

B. JACKSON and D. MARSDEN, *Education and the Working Class*. Routledge & Kegan Paul. 1962.

H. JENNINGS, *Societies in the Making*. Routledge & Kegan Paul. 1962.

P. JEPHCOTT with N. SEEAR and J. H. SMITH, *Married Women Working*. George Allen & Unwin. 1962.

M. KERR, *Personality and Conflict in Jamaica*. Liverpool University Press. 1952.

M. KERR, *The People of Ship Street*. Routledge & Kegan Paul. 1958.

W. I. N. KESSEL, 'Psychiatric Morbidity in a London General Practice.' *British Journal of Preventive and Social Medicine,* Vol. 14, No. 1. 1960.

W. I. N. KESSEL and M. SHEPHERD, 'Neurosis in Hospital and General Practice.' *Journal of Mental Science,* Vol. 108, No. 453. 1962.

C. KIRKPATRICK, *The Family as Process and Institution*. Ronald Press, New York. 1955.

J. KLEIN, *Samples from English Cultures*. Routledge & Kegan Paul. 1965.

V. KLEIN, *Britain's Married Women Workers*. Routledge & Kegan Paul. 1965.

V. KLEIN, *Employing Married Women*. Institute of Personnel Management. Occasional Papers, No. 17. 1961.

Bibliography

V. KLEIN, *The Emancipation of Women: Its Motives and Achievements.* In: *Ideas and Beliefs of the Victorians* (B.B.C. Talks). Sylvan Press. 1949.

V. KLEIN, *Working Wives.* Institute of Personnel Management. Occasional Papers, No. 15. 1958.

M. KOHN, 'Social Class and Parent Child Relationships. An Interpretation.' *American Journal of Sociology*, Vol. 68, No. 4. 1963.

E. L. KOOS, *Families in Trouble.* Kings Crown Press, New York. 1946.

A. KORNHAUSER and P. B. SHEATSLEY, 'Questionnaire Construction and Interview Procedure.' From: C. Sellitz, M. Jahoda, M. Deutsch, S. Cook, *Research Methods in Social Relations.* Methuen. 1962.

P. LASLETT, 'Social Change in England 1901–51.' *The Listener*, Vol. LXVI, No. 1709. 1961.

P. LASLETT, 'What is so Special About Us Now.' *The Listener*, Vol. LXIX, No. 1767. 1963.

D. LOCKWOOD, 'The New Working Class.' *Archives Européennes de Sociologie*, Vol. 1, No. 2. 1960.

E. E. and N. MACCOBY, 'The Interview.' In: G. Lindzey (Ed.), *Handbook of Social Psychology.* Addison Wesley Mass. 1954.

O. R. MCGREGOR and G. ROWNTREE, 'The Family.' In: A. T. Welford, M. Argyle, D. V. Glass, J. N. Morris (Eds.), *Society. Problems and Methods of Study.* Routledge & Kegan Paul. 1962.

O. R. MCGREGOR, 'The Stability of the Family in the Welfare State.' *The Political Quarterly*, Vol. 31, No. 2. April 1960.

R. M. MACIVER and C. H. PAGE, *Society.* Macmillan. 1949.

J. MAIZELS, *Two to Five in High Flats.* Joseph Rowntree Memorial Trust. 1961.

J. B. MAYS, *Education and the Urban Child.* Liverpool University Press. 1962.

R. K. MERTON and P. L. KENDALL, 'The Focussed Interview.' *American Journal of Sociology*, Vol. 4, No. 6. 1946.

D. MILLER and G. SWANSON, *The Changing American Parent.* John Wiley & Sons, New York. 1958.

F. J. W. MILLER, S. D. M. COURT, W. S. WALTON and E. G. KNOX, *Growing Up in Newcastle on Tyne.* Oxford University Press. 1960.

Bibliography

J. M. MOGEY, *Family and Neighbourhood*. Oxford University Press. 1956.

A. MYRDAL and V. KLEIN, *Women's Two Roles*. Routledge & Kegan Paul. 1956.

S. F. NADEL, *The Theory of Social Structure*. Cohen & West. 1957.

S. F. NADEL, *New Society*, 'The Rewards of Training Women.' Vol. 1, No. 11. 1962.

J. and E. NEWSON, *Infant Care in an Urban Community*. George Allen & Unwin. 1963.

T. PARSONS and R. F. BALES, *Family: Socialisation and Interaction Process*. Routledge & Kegan Paul. 1955.

T. PARSONS, 'General Theory in Sociology.' From: R. K. Merton, L. Brown, L. S. Cottrell, Jr., *Sociology Today*. Basic Books, New York. 1959.

I. PINCHBECK, *Women Workers and the Industrial Revolution*. George Routledge & Sons. 1930.

POLITICAL AND ECONOMIC PLANNING, *Family Needs and the Social Structure*. George Allen & Unwin. 1961.

D. A. POND, A. RYLE and M. HAMILTON, 'Marriage and Neurosis in a Working Class Population.' *British Journal of Psychiatry*, Vol. 109, No. 462. 1963.

E. RATHBONE, *The Harvest of the Women's Movement*. Fawcett Lecture, Bedford College. 1935.

A. READ (Ed.), *The First Five Years of Marriage*. National Marriage Guidance Council. 1963.

M. PEMBER REEVES, *Round About a Pound a Week*. G. Bell & Sons. 1913.

REGISTRAR GENERAL, *Statistical Review of England & Wales 1956*, Part III, Commentary. H.M.S.O. 1958.

REGISTRAR GENERAL, *Statistical Review of England & Wales 1960*, Part III, Commentary. H.M.S.O. 1962.

REGISTRAR GENERAL, *Statistical Review of England & Wales 1962*. H.M.S.O. 1964.

REPORT OF THE CENTRAL ADVISORY COUNCIL FOR EDUCATION, *Fifteen to Eighteen* (The Crowther Report). H.M.S.O. 1960.

REPORT OF THE NATIONAL FOOD SURVEY COMMITTEE 1952, *Domestic Food Consumption and Expenditure*. H.M.S.O. 1954.

G. ROWNTREE, 'New Facts on Teenage Marriage.' *New Society*, Vol. I, No. 1. 1962.

G. ROWNTREE and N. H. CARRIER, 'The Resort to Divorce in

England & Wales 1858–1957.' *Population Studies,* Vol. XI, No. 3. 1958.

G. ROWNTREE and R. M. PIERCE, 'Birth Control in Britain,' Part 1. *Population Studies,* Vol. XV, No. 1. 1961.

THE ROYAL COMMISSION ON POPULATION. H.M.S.O. 1949.

A. RYLE and M. HAMILTON, 'Neurosis in Fifty Married Couples.' *Journal of Mental Science,* Vol. 108, No. 454. 1962.

SALES RESEARCH SERVICES, 'Why do Housewives Go Out to Work?' *New Society,* Vol. I, No. 26. 1963.

N. SEEAR, 'Womanpower Needs a Policy.' *New Society,* Vol. I, No. 9. 1962.

N. SEEAR, V. ROBERTS and J. BROCK, *A Career for Women in Industry.* Oliver & Boyd. 1964.

C. SELLITZ, M. JAHODA, M. DEUTSCH and S. COOK. *Research Methods in Social Relations.* Methuen. 1962.

L. A. SHAW. 'Impressions of Family Life in a London Suburb.' *The Sociological Review,* New Series Vol. 2, No. 2. December 1954.

E. SLATER and M. WOODSIDE, *Patterns of Marriage.* Cassell. 1951.

B. SPINLEY, *The Deprived and the Privileged.* Routledge & Kegan Paul. 1953.

M. SPRING-RICE, *Working Class Wives.* Pelican Books. 1939.

C. M. STEWART, 'Future Trends in the Employment of Married Women.' *British Journal of Sociology,* Vol. XII, No. 1. 1961.

M. B. SUSSMAN, 'The Help Pattern in the Middle Class Family.' *American Sociological Review,* Vol. 18, No. 1. March 1953.

B. THOMPSON and A. FINLAYSON, 'Married Women Who Work in Early Motherhood.' *British Journal of Sociology,* Vol. 14, No. 2. 1963.

R. M. TITMUSS, *Essays on the Welfare State.* George Allen & Unwin. 1958.

P. TOWNSEND, *The Family Life of Old People.* Routledge & Kegan Paul. 1960.

T. VENESS, *School Leavers.* Methuen. 1962.

C. VEREKER and J. B. MAYS, *Urban Redevelopment and Social Change.* Liverpool University Press. 1961.

P. WILLMOTT, *The Evolution of a Community.* Routledge & Kegan Paul. 1963.

B. WILSON, 'The Teachers' Role.' *British Journal of Sociology,* Vol. XIII, No. 1. 1962.

R. WILSON. 'Difficult Housing Estates.' *Human Relations*, Vol. 16, No. 1. 1963.

M. WOLLSTONECRAFT, *A Vindication of the Rights of Women*. Walter Scott. 1792.

WOMEN'S CO-OPERATIVE GUILD, *Maternity—Letters from Working Women*. G. Bell & Sons. 1915.

B. WOOTTON, *Social Science and Social Pathology*. George Allen & Unwin. 1959.

M. YOUNG and P. WILLMOTT, *Family and Kinship in East London*. Routledge & Kegan Paul. 1957.

S. YUDKIN and A. HOLME, *Working Mothers and Their Children*. Michael Joseph. 1963.

C. C. ZIMMERMAN, *The Family and Civilisation*. Harper, New York. 1947.

TAYA ZINKIN, 'Women Talking.' *The Guardian*. 8th July 1963.

F. ZWEIG, *The Worker in an Affluent Society*. Heinemann. 1961.

F. ZWEIG, *Women's Life and Labour*. Gollancz. 1952.

ADDITIONAL BIBLIOGRAPHY

BARRETT, M. (1980), *Women's Oppression Today*, London, Verso Editions.

DE BEAUVOIR, S. (1949), *The Second Sex* (Harmondsworth, Penguin edition, 1972).

DAVIDOFF, L. (1973), *The Best Circles*, London, Croom Helm.

DAVIDSON, C. (1982), *A Woman's Work is Never Done*, London, Chatto & Windus.

FENSTERMAKER BERK, S. (1980), *Women and Household Labor*, Beverly Hills, Sage Publications.

FRIEDAN, B. (1963), *The Feminine Mystique*, New York, W. W. Norton.

GINSBERG, S. (1976), 'Women, Work and Conflict', in N. Fonda and P. Moss (eds), *Mothers in Employment*, Brunel University.

HOBSON, D. (1978), 'Housewives: Isolation as Oppression', in *Women Take Issue*, The Women's Studies Group, Centre for Contemporary Cultural Studies, University of Birmingham; London, Hutchinson.

KLEIN, V. (1946), *The Feminine Character*, London, Kegan Paul, Trench and Trubner.

Bibliography

KOMAROVSKY, M. (1953), *Women in the Modern World: their education and their dilemmas*, Boston, Little Brown.

LOPATA, H. (1971), *Occupation Housewife*, New York, Oxford University Press.

LUXTON, M. (1980), *More Than a Labour of Love*, Toronto, The Women's Press.

MCBRIDE, T. (1976), *The Domestic Revolution*, London, Croom Helm.

MCKEE, L. (1982), 'Fathers' Participation in Infant Care: a critique', in L. McKee and M. O'Brien (eds), *The Father Figure*, London, Tavistock.

OAKLEY, A. (1974a), *The Sociology of Housework*, London, Martin Robertson.

OAKLEY, A. (1974b), *Housewife*, Harmondsworth, Allen Lane.

PIERCY, M. (1979), *Woman on the Edge of Time*, London, The Women's Press.

SECOMBE, W. (1973), 'The Housewife and her Labour under Capitalism', *New Left Review* 83.

STRASSER, S. (1982), *Never Done*, New York, Pantheon.

THOMPSON, E. (1978), *The Poverty of Theory and Other Essays*, London, Merlin Press.

WILSON, E. (1980), *Only Halfway to Paradise*, London, Tavistock.

ZARETSKY, E. (1976), *Capitalism, the Family and Personal Life*, New York, Harper & Row.

INDEX